THE
LOST APOCRYPHA OF
THE OLD TESTAMENT

THEIR TITLES AND FRAGMENTS

COLLECTED, TRANSLATED, AND DISCUSSED

BY

MONTAGUE RHODES JAMES

LITT.D., F.B.A., F.S.A.
HON. LITT.D. DUBLIN ; HON. L.L.D. ST. ANDREWS
PROVOST OF ETON COLLEGE ; SOMETIME PROVOST
OF KING'S COLLEGE, CAMBRIDGE

THE BOOK TREE
San Diego, California

Originally published
1920
by THE MACMILLAN COMPANY
New York

ISBN 978-1-58509- 269-7

Published by
The Book Tree
P.O. Box 16476
San Diego, CA 92176
www.thebooktree.com

We provide fascinating and educational products to help awaken the public to new ideas and
information that would not be available otherwise.
Call 1 (800) 700-8733 for our *FREE BOOK TREE CATALOG.*

FOREWORD

There are many ancient, lost books relating to the Bible and this work covers the ones that are most hard to find, dating between 100 BCE and 100 CE. In many cases we do not have the full works, but have various sections and fragments. The author, Montague James, used quotations found mostly in the works of the Greek Ante-Nicene Fathers like Origen, Hippolytus and Clement of Alexandria to piece together what we are missing. He also uses important lists compiled from Greek, Latin and other languages in order to reveal what we know of other missing books that would, in some cases, otherwise be unheard of. This important piece of scholarship should be part of anyone's library who is seriously researching lost and ancient texts.

CONTENTS

CONTENTS

INTRODUCTORY

THE SOURCES.—PATRISTIC QUOTATIONS

THE object of this book is to collect in a form convenient to English readers the remains of some of the apocryphal writings connected with the Old Testament which have not survived in their entirety. That there were many such books we know; and the student may find, scattered in dictionary articles, or collected in such works as the—still unsurpassed—*Codex Pseudepigraphus Veteris Testamenti* of John Albert Fabricius, their names and fragments. But there is not a handy English guide to this information, such as I now attempt to supply.

It is impossible in most cases to assign anything like a precise date to these writings; the most we can say is that they are pre- or post-Christian (and even that is not always clear), and that they must have been in existence before the time of the writer who quotes them. That latter point at least is certain. But we shall not be far out if we regard the first century before and the first century after the Christian era (100 B.C.–A.D. 100) as covering the period during which most of them were produced. Our uncertainty as to their chronological order forbids me to attempt any arrangement of them based upon date; and I have preferred the simpler plan of following the Biblical order of the personages to whom they are attributed, or of whom they treat.

Before, however, we consider any of them individually, it will be well to form an idea of the sources from which we get any information about them.

These are mainly of two kinds : lists of books, and quotations.

The quotations from these books are for the most part to be found in the writings of the Greek Ante-Nicene Fathers. The so-called Apostolic Fathers, Clement of Rome, Barnabas, and Hermas, are important contributors; Justin Martyr and the other apologists give us little. Clement of Alexandria and Origen are incomparably the richest sources; Hippolytus has something. In the fourth century the yield is far smaller : Epiphanius, a determined borrower from earlier writers, is not to be despised; but for our present purpose such writers as Athanasius, Basil, Chrysostom, the Gregories, are barren and useless. The next stratum that is at all productive (and the last) is to be found in the Byzantine chronographers, George the Syncellus, George Cedrenus, Michael Glycas.

The Latins are throughout poorer. Tertullian and Cyprian will be referred to; but Jerome hates apocryphal literature, and says so, while Augustine, a valuable source of knowledge about some New Testament Apocrypha, never, it so happens, quotes spurious Old Testament literature at all. Yet, if Latin Fathers are poor, we shall see that Latin versions of some very queer books were current, and have left traces in manuscripts.

PRODUCTION OF APOCRYPHA

We can readily understand, or at least imagine, the state of mind which made the later Church writers chary of quoting the extra-canonical books. For one thing, the conception of canonicity had grown much clearer by the fourth century; the experience of the first three centuries had shown the necessity of defining doctrine, and consequently of stating clearly what books purporting to be sacred were really to be considered authoritative, and could legitimately be used in public worship. Most of us have very little idea how many gospels, revelations, histories or " acts " of apostles, and books of prophecies were in circulation for which the claim was set up that they should be so used. It was the recognized method of pushing a particular set of doctrines to produce a writing under some venerable name, in which the special tenets were openly or covertly advocated. The fashion is on the wane now, yet we have heard of the *Book of Mormon*, of Notovich's Buddhist *Life of Christ*, and perhaps of an astounding work called the *Archko Volume*. But though the methods of to-day are of necessity different, it would not be very surprising even now if a coterie of spiritualists were to publish, and to gain some credence for, a Life of our Lord dictated " automatically " by the spirit of one who had known Him in the flesh; and this war has taught us that apocryphal prophecies are by no means out of date.

It was, of course, specially important that the books which professed to contain teachings of Christ or of Apostles should be sifted; but it was also necessary to banish from the churches those which had been fathered upon the prophets and patriarchs of the Old Testament. Many such had been made the vehicle of anti-Catholic, and even of anti-Christian, teaching. We shall encounter instances of these, though they are not so common as writings that are legendary, or apocalyptic.

LISTS AND STICHOMETRIES

This necessity for definition led to the drawing-up of lists of the sacred books, and then, naturally, of longer lists, in which apocryphal books were included and expressly reprobated. Such lists form our second main source of knowledge about the lost writings. There are three Greek lists, one Latin, and some in other languages, especially Armenian, which will have to be noticed.

The Greek lists are known as the Stichometry of Nicephorus, the list of the Sixty Books, and that in the Pseudo-Athanasian *Synopsis of Holy Scripture*. The Stichometry of Nicephorus is a catalogue appended to the chronography called of Nicephorus, Patriarch of Constantinople (806–815), and it is called " Stichometry " because it appends to the title of each book a statement of the number of *stichoi* or lines which it contained. The line was the unit of payment for the professional scribe, and was commonly of the average length of a line of Homer, say sixteen syllables or thirty-four to thirty-six letters. It is thought that this particular catalogue must be appreciably older than the ninth century, perhaps as old as the fifth or sixth; but I do not think its date is very important to us. It seems to have been added to the chronography about 850, at Jerusalem. The list in the *Synopsis of Scripture*, falsely attributed to Athanasius, is very similar to that of Nicephorus, but not, in the judgment of a good critic, Theodor Zahn, copied from it. In the single section which concerns us, the two are identical. The book in which it occurs is of uncertain date, not earlier than the sixth century.

The list of the Sixty Books is found appended in some MSS., but not in all, to the *Quæstiones* of Anastasius of Sinai. By the Sixty Books the Canonical Scriptures are meant. The names of these are followed by nine more, described as "outside the Sixty" (Wisdom, Ecclus., 1–4 Macc., Esther, Judith, Tobit), and these by twenty-four more under the title "apocrypha." Probably this list also may be of the sixth or seventh century.

The three lists contain the following titles of Old Testament apocryphal books :—

Nicephorus (Synopsis)	No. of lines.[1]	Sixty Books.
Enoch	4800	Adam.
Patriarchs	5100	Enoch.
Prayer of Joseph	1100	Lamech.
Testament of Moses	1100	Patriarchs.
Assumption of Moses	1400	Prayer of Joseph.
Abraham	300	Eldad and Modad.
Eldad and Modad	400	Testament of Moses.
Of Elias the Prophet	316	Assumption of Moses.
Of Sophonias the Prophet	600	Psalms of Solomon.
Of Zacharias the father		Apocalypse of Elias.
of John	500	Vision of Esaias.
Pseudepigrapha of Baruch,		Apocalypse of Sophonias.
Ambacum (Habakkuk),		Apocalypse of Zacharias.
Ezekiel, and Daniel		Apocalypse of Esdras.

[1] In *Nicephorus* only.

The Latin list of apocryphal books is contained in a document known as the *Gelasian Decree*, " concerning books to be received and not to be received." It purports to have been issued by a Pope acting as the mouthpiece of a Council of bishops; in most MSS. the Pope is Gelasius I (496), but in some Damasus (384), and in some Hormisdas (523). The view expressed by its latest editor, E. von Dobschütz, is that it is not really a papal document at all, but a compilation made in France in the sixth century. That question is not settled. Whatever its origin, the *Decree* gives us several very unusual names of apocryphal books, and omits many, like *Enoch*, which we should expect to find, and which we know were current in Latin. Its contribution is as follows :—

The book, concerning the daughters of Adam, of Leptogenesis . . . . Apocryphal.
The book which is called the Penitence of Adam . . . . . . Apocryphal.
The book concerning the giant named Ogias, who is stated by the heretics to have fought with a dragon after the Flood . . Apocryphal.
The book which is called the Testament of Job . . . . . . Apocryphal.
The book which is called the Penitence of Jannes and Mambres . . . Apocryphal.
The writing which is called the Interdiction (*or* Contradiction) of Solomon . Apocryphal.

The Armenian lists collected by Zahn in 1893 (*Forschungen*, V. 109) are three in number.

1. Samuel of Ani (*cir.* 1179) mentions, among books brought into Armenia about A.D. 591 by Nestorian missionaries, the *Penitence of Adam*, and the *Testament ;* the latter may be that of Moses, but is more probably that of Adam.

2. Mechithar of Aïrivank (*cir.* 1290) has a list closely resembling the Greek ones. One section of it is headed *Secret Books of the Jews*, and runs thus :—

(1) Book of Adam.
(2) Book of Enoch.

(3) Book of the Sibyl.

(4) The twelve Patriarchs, *i. e.* the testaments of the twelve sons of Jacob.

(5) The Prayers of Joseph.

(6) The Ascension of Moses.

(7) Eldad, Modad.

(8) The Psalms of Solomon.

(9) The Mysteries of Elias.

(10) The Seventh Vision of Daniel.

This is essentially the list of the Sixty Books, substituting the *Sibyl* for *Lamech*, omitting the *Testament of Moses*, and replacing the last four items by the *Seventh Vision of Daniel*.

3. A second list in the same writer's chronicle, under the year 1085, mingles some apocryphal titles with the Canon of the Old Testament, viz. :—

The Vision of Enok—probably a late document (translated by Issaverdens).

The Testaments of the Patriarchs.

The Prayers of Aseneth.

Tobit, Judith, Esther.

Ezdras Salathiel (*i. e.* 4 Esdras).

(Job, etc.).

The Paralipomena concerning Jeremiah Babylon (*i. e.* the Rest of the Words of Baruch).

Deaths of the Prophets (a version of the Pseudo-Epiphanian Lives of the Prophets).

Jesus Sirac.

This list consists entirely of books which still exist. The *Prayers of Aseneth* seems to take the place of the *Prayer of Joseph* in the former list.

The above lists include nearly all the names which will concern us. Some notice, however, will have to be taken of other writings attributed to some of those whose names occur in the lists, *e. g.* Moses, and of books fathered upon, or relating to, Eve, Seth, Noah, Ham, Melchizedek, Hezekiah, as well as the ancient Persian king Hystaspes; and a collection of the passages which early writers have quoted without naming their source.

THE LOST APOCRYPHA OF
THE OLD TESTAMENT

THE FRAGMENTS

ADAM

WE hear of quite a considerable number of books attributed to, or relating to, Adam : an *Apocalypse*, a *Penitence*, a *Testament*, a *Life*, are the foremost. As to the first three of these titles, there is uncertainty as to whether they represent one, two, or three books. Perhaps it will be possible to form an opinion when the evidence has been set out.

The *Apocalypse of Adam* is expressly and certainly quoted only once.

In the *Epistle of Barnabas*, ii. 10, we read: " But to us he speaks thus : ' The sacrifice of God is a contrite heart ; a savour of sweetness to the Lord is a heart glorifying Him that hath formed it.' " Upon this the Constantinople MS. has this marginal note : " Psalm l. and in the *Apocalypse of Adam*." The first clause is, of course, familiar, occurring in Ps. l. (li.) ; the second is not from the Bible. Yet two early Fathers, namely, Clement of Alexandria and Irenæus, quote it in this form—Clement twice—always in connexion with the passage Isa. i. 11, which, be it noted, Barnabas has also quoted just before. We need not doubt the statement that the words occurred in the *Apocalypse of Adam*. They have to do with repentance, and plainly repentance was a favourite topic in connexion with Adam. The *Gelasian Decree* and an Armenian list, we have seen, mention a *Penitence of Adam.* In the Gnostic book called the *Pistis Sophia,* by the way, the word *penitence* has a technical meaning; it is applied to the hymns sung by the being Pistis Sophia on her progress through the spiritual world; each hymn is called " a penitence."

Further, we have another passage which connects together the ideas of repentance and of a revelation made to Adam. George Cedrenus, a Byzantine chronicler, says (ed. Migne, i. 41) : " Adam, in the 600th year, having repented, learned by revelation concerning the Watchers and the Flood and concerning repentance and the divine incarnation, and concerning the prayers that are sent up to God by all creatures at every hour of the day and night, by the hand of Uriel, the angel that is over repentance. In the first hour of the day the first prayer is accomplished in heaven, in the second hour is the prayer of angels, in the third the prayer of winged things, in the fourth the prayer of cattle, in the fifth the prayer of wild beasts, in the sixth the assembly (*or* review) of angels and the discerning (*or* inspection) of all creation, in the seventh the entering in of angels to God and their going out, in the eighth the praise and sacrifices of angels, in the ninth the prayer and worship of men, in the tenth the visitations of waters and the prayers of things in heaven and on earth, in the eleventh the thanksgiving and rejoicing of all things, in the twelfth the entreatings of men unto well-pleasing." He goes on : " And in the 950th year Adam died, on the very day of his transgression, and returned unto the earth from whence he was taken, leaving thirty-three sons and twenty-three daughters."

This horary of the day, and also that of the night, we possess in various other forms. One is in Greek, and has survived under the name, not of Adam, but of Apollonius (of Tyana), the famous thaumaturge of the first century. The latest editor of it, Abbé F. Nau (in *Patrologia Syriaca,* i. 2, Appendix, 1907), is of opinion that it may really be attributed to Apollonius or his circle, and that it was transferred from his book to that of Adam ; but his case is a weak one : the text is full of

Christian touches, and the evidence that it was originally under Adam's name is earlier in date than any
that can be produced for Apollonius.

The horary seems also to have been known in the
Latin Church. Nicetas of Remesiana, writing in the
fourth century *On the Merit of Psalmody*, has this
sentence: " We ought not rashly to receive the book
that is entitled the Inquisition of Abraham, wherein it
is feigned that the very animals, springs, and elements
sang, inasmuch as that book is of no credit and rests
on no authority." I conjecture (and others agree) that
Inquisition of Abraham (*Inquisitio Abræ*) is a corruption of *Dispositio* (*i. e.* Testament) *Adæ*.

We have it also in Syriac, where it is said to be from
the *Testament of Adam*. There are two Syriac versions,
edited and translated by Kmosko, in the volume of the
Patrologia Syriaca referred to above. One of these has
this introductory note: " When he was sick unto death,
he called Seth his son, and said to him : My son, He
that formed me out of the dust showed me and granted
me to put names upon the beasts of the earth and the
fowls of heaven, and showed me the hours of the day
and night, how they stand."

And more than once Adam speaks in the first person,
e. g. at the fourth hour of the night: " The Trisagion
of the Seraphim : thus I used to hear, my son, before
I sinned, the sound of their wings in Paradise, and after
I had transgressed the commandment I heard it not."

There is thus a prima facie case for thinking that the
Apocalypse, Penitence, and *Testament of Adam*, if not
identical, at least contained a good deal of common
matter.

The Syriac MSS. of the horary, or some of them,
append to it other passages which purport to come from
the *Testament*. One of these is a prophecy of the
coming of Christ, addressed to Seth. Of this we have
two texts, the second very much amplified. After the
prophecy is another prediction that a flood will come
because of the sin of Cain, and that the world will last
6000 years after that. Then follows the statement :

B

"I, Seth, wrote this testament: Adam died and was buried on the east of Paradise, over against the first city that was built, named Henoch. He was buried by the angels, and the sun and moon were darkened seven days. Seth sealed the Testament and laid it up in the Cave of Treasures with the gold, frankincense, and myrrh which Adam brought out of Paradise, and which the Magi are to offer to the Son of God in Bethlehem of Judah."

This, of course, is throughout Christian, and the mention of the Cave of Treasures links it up with a whole series of Eastern books, such as the *Book of Adam and Eve* (tr. S. C. Malan), the *Cave of Treasures* (ed. Bezold), the *Book of the Rolls* (Gibson, *Studia Sinaitica*, viii.).

The last fragment has really no claim to be connected with Adam at all. It is an account of the nine orders of angels in which there is mention of David, Zechariah, and Judas Maccabæus.

If the horary and the prophecy were parts of the same book, it was a Christian, or at least a fully Christianized text, and not a very early one. Yet I find it difficult not to suspect the existence of an early book behind it. The last words of Tertullian's book *On Penitence* seem to imply that he knew of some writing in which Adam's praises of God after his repentance were recorded. He says: "For, since I am a sinner of the deepest dye, and not born for any end except repentance, I cannot easily keep silence about it (*i. e.* repentance), and no more does Adam—the beginner both of the race of men and of sin against the Lord—when by confession he has been restored unto his Paradise." No more may be meant than that Adam, now that he is redeemed and restored, sings praise to God; but the other view has usually been taken, and if it is correct it means that there was in the second century a book that contained hymns uttered by Adam after his fall and repentance. The phrase quoted from the *Epistle of Barnabas* might well be a fragment of such a writing.

Certain it is that legend was busy with accounts of

the penitence of Adam : of the attempt made by him and Eve to do penance apart for forty days in the waters of the Tigris and Euphrates—an attempt frustrated by Satan, who disguised himself as an angel and induced Eve to come out of the water on the pretence that God had forgiven and forgotten all. This story appears both in the Eastern *Book* (*or Conflict*) *of Adam and Eve*, and in the Latin *Life of Adam*. The common source of these widely divergent streams must lie far behind both.

The *Life of Adam* has been mentioned. In some form it has made its way into most of the vernaculars of Europe, usually by means of the Latin version, which is common in MSS. from the ninth to the fifteenth century. It and its elder sister, or parent, the Greek, may be read in English in Charles's *Pseudepigrapha*, and I need not analyze either further than to say that the Greek and Latin both contain detailed accounts of the Fall, and of the Death and Burial of Adam, while the Latin also has, as noted above, something about his Penitence. But these were not the only Lives of Adam that were current. A text of a different kind is quoted by George Syncellus in his *Chronography*, p. 5. He says : I have been necessitated (by the silence of the canonical Scriptures, he means) to give some explanation of this matter (*i. e.* the dates of Adam's life), such as other historians of Jewish antiquities and Christian history have recorded out of the *Leptogenesis* (*i. e.* the *Book of Jubilees*) and the so-called *Life of Adam*— though they may not seem authoritative—lest those interested in such questions should fall into extravagant opinions. In the so-called *Life of Adam*, then, is set forth both the number of the days of the naming of the beasts, and that of the creation of the woman and of the entrance of Adam himself into Paradise, and of the precept of God to him about the eating of the tree, and of the entry of Eve into Paradise with him, and the story of the Fall and what followed it, as is subjoined.

"On the 1st day of the week, which was the 3rd day

of the creation of Adam and the 8th of the 1st month
Nisan, and the 1st of the month of April, and 6th of the
Egyptian month Pharmouthi, Adam by a divine gift
of grace named the wild beasts. On the 2nd day of the
2nd week he named the cattle; on the 3rd day of
the 2nd week he named the fowls; on the 4th day of the
2nd week he named the creeping things; on the 5th
day of the 2nd week he named those that swim. On
the 6th day of the 2nd week, which was, according to the
Romans, the 6th of April, and according to the Egyptians
the 11th of Pharmouthi, God took a part of the rib of
Adam and formed the woman.

  " On the 46th day of the creation of the world, the
4th day of the 7th week, the 14th of Pachon, and 9th
of May, the sun being in Taurus and the moon diametric-
ally opposite in Scorpius, at the rising of the Pleiads,
God brought Adam into Paradise on the 40th day from
his creation.

  " On the 50th day of the creation of the world, and
44th of that of Adam, being Sunday the 18th of Pachon
and 13th of May, three days after his entry into Paradise,
the sun being in Taurus and the moon in Capricorn,
God commanded Adam to abstain from eating of the
tree of knowledge.

  " On the 93rd day of the creation, the 2nd day of the
46th week, at the summer solstice, the sun and moon
being in Cancer, on the 25th of the month of June and
1st of Epiphi, Eve the helpmeet of Adam was brought
by God into Paradise, on the 80th day of her creation,
and Adam took her and named her Eve, which is interpreted Life. Therefore God ordained by Moses in
Leviticus, on account of the days of the separation (of
Eve from Adam) after her creation, out of Paradise,
that the woman should be unclean 40 days after the
birth of a male child, and 80 days after the birth of a
female. For Adam was brought into Paradise on the
40th day of his creation, wherefore also they bring male
children into the Temple on the 40th day according to
the Law. But for a female child she is to be unclean
80 days, both because Eve entered into Paradise on the

8oth day, and also because of the impureness of the female compared with the male; for when she is unclean she does not enter the Temple until 7 days after, according to the Law of God.

"This we have copied shortly out of the so-called *Life of Adam* for the information of students."

Now, although George Syncellus expressly distinguishes the *Leptogenesis* (*Book of Jubilees*) from the *Life of Adam*, and subsequently gives quotations avowedly made from it, the fact remains that practically all that he quotes from the *Life of Adam* occurs in *Jubilees* (iii. 1–11). The month-reckonings and the astronomical details are not there, but all the facts are. It has been held that the *Life* was an amplified episode taken from *Jubilees*, or that it is merely another name for *Jubilees*. The former is to my mind the more likely explanation, for there is another bit of evidence in favour of the separate existence of such a writing. Anastasius of Sinai, writing at the end of the sixth century, says (*on the Hexæmeron*, vii. p. 895): "The Hebrews assert, on the authority of a book not-included in the Canon, which is called the *Testament of the Protoplasts*, that Adam entered Paradise on the 40th day, and that is the view also of a historian, the chronographer Pyrrho, and of many commentators."

This *Testament* may very well have been the same as Syncellus's *Life*. I think we need not greatly regret that we do not possess this *Life* or *Testament*: we probably have most of the matter of it either in *Jubilees* or in the Greek and Latin texts I have described.

The *Apocalypse-Testament* would have been more interesting, with its hymns of the repentant Adam and the Messianic predictions which I do not doubt that it contained. One more testimony to its existence must be put on record. Epiphanius (*Heresy*, 26), treating of the "Borborite" Gnostics, makes (in § 5) this quotation: "Reading in apocryphal writings that 'I saw a tree bearing twelve fruits in the year, and he said to me, " This is the tree of life," ' the heretics interpret it " in a way which need not be remembered. Later on (in § 8) he says that they use "Apocalypses of Adam" as well as other spurious books. The plural is merely rhetorical. It has been assumed, plausibly enough, that the quotation about the tree—which nearly coincides with Rev. xxii. 2—is from the *Apocalypse of Adam ;* but this is no more than an assumption. The importance of the passage is that it gives fourth-century evidence of the currency of the Apocalypse.

Upon the whole I incline (in spite of the evidence of Samuel of Ani) to the opinion that there were two outstanding Adam-books of Jewish origin. One, the *Apocalypse* (*Testament, Penitence*), which is gone, except for a few quotations ; the other the *Life*, which is represented in its main features by the Latin and Greek texts (*Vita Adæ et Evæ*, and *" Apocalypse of Moses"*).

EVE

The only book current under this name was a " Gospel," and Epiphanius is the only authority for its existence. In the same 26th *Heresy* (2, 3) he says : " Others do not scruple to speak of a *Gospel of Eve*, for they father their offspring upon her name, as supposedly the discoverer of the food of knowledge by revelation of the serpent that spake to her." " Their words," he goes on, " like those of a drunkard, are fit to move sometimes laughter, sometimes tears. They deal in foolish visions and testimonies in this Gospel of theirs." Thus : " I stood upon a high mountain, and I saw a tall man and another, a short man, and I heard as it were the voice of thunder, and drew near to hearken, and he spake to me and said : ' I am thou and thou art I. And wheresoever thou art, there am I, and I am dispersed among all things, and whence thou wilt thou canst gather me, and in gathering me thou gatherest thyself.' " This is pantheistic stuff, of a kind, one would suppose, very easy to write, if a model were furnished. I give it a place here only for the sake of completeness : it is no more an Old Testament apocryph than it is a gospel.

SETH

Seth was in like manner the ostensible author of many Gnostic books. But there is a passage both in Syncellus and Cedrenus which deserves to be quoted as possibly preserving a notice of a lost writing under his name, of less eccentric character. I quote Cedrenus (ed. Migne, col. 8) : " Seth is recorded as the third son of Adam. He married his own sister, called Asouam, and begat Enos. Seth signifies resurrection. He was also called God, because of the shining of his face, which lasted all his life. Moses also had this grace, and so veiled himself when he spoke with the Jews, for forty years. Seth gave names to the seven planets, and comprehended the lore of the movements of the heavens. He also prepared two pillars, one of stone and one of brick, and wrote these things upon them." (The rest of this familiar story from Josephus is then given.) " He also devised the Hebrew letters. Now Seth was born in the 230th year of Adam, and was weaned when he was twelve years old, and in the 270th year of Adam Seth was caught away by an angel and instructed in what concerned the future transgression of his sons (that is to say, the Watchers, who were also called Sons of God), and concerning the Flood and the coming of the Saviour. And on the fortieth day after he had disappeared, he returned and told the protoplasts all that he had been taught by the angel. He was comely and well-formed, both he and those that were born of him, who were called Watchers and Sons of God because of the shining of the face of Seth. And they dwelt on the higher land of Eden near to Paradise, living the life of angels, until the 1000th year of the world."

Dr. Charles may be right in regarding this statement (about the revelations made to Seth) as an attempt to transfer to him the wisdom and the position which properly belonged to Enoch. Still, there is evidence, at any rate, of Messianic prophecies attributed to Seth, besides those which Adam revealed to him, and which are recorded in the fragments of the *Testament*, and more shortly in the *Life*.

In particular, the Arian author of a commentary on St. Matthew, printed with the works of St. Chrysostom and known as the *Opus Imperfectum*, quotes a story about the Magi, "among whom (in their own country) was current a writing inscribed with the name of Seth, concerning the star which was to appear and the gifts that were to be offered to Christ." In the Armenian *Gospel of the Infancy*, translated into French by P. Peeters (1914), the Magi are represented as bringing with them a Messianic prophecy by Adam which Seth had received and handed on to his posterity. These are, of course, Christian compositions, and not necessarily or probably of early date.

LAMECH

Lamech is the next title in the lists of Apocryphal books which concerns us. There are two antediluvians of the name recorded in Genesis : in iv. 25 ff. we have the descendant of Cain, the author of the Song; in v. 25 ff. the descendant of Seth and father of Noah. The former has been the subject of more legend than the latter. The enigmatical Song has had explanations invented for it, of which that which has attained the widest currency is as follows. Lamech was blind, and used to go out shooting with bow and arrow under the guidance of the young Tubal Cain. The function of Tubal was to tell the old man where the game was, and direct his shot. One day Tubal was aware of something moving in the thicket; he turned Lamech's aim upon it, and the creature fell dead. It proved to be their ancestor Cain—covered with hair and with a horn growing out of his forehead—for such was the mark set upon him by God. Lamech, on learning what he had done, smote his mighty hands together in consternation, and in so doing smote and slew Tubal Cain. Thus it was that he "killed a man to his wounding and a young man to his hurt."

This tale is current in a separate form in Slavonic.

No one has made a better conjecture than that the lost book of Lamech had this for its principal subject. Many are the Jewish writers and mediæval Western commentators who tell the story, and through the medium of the latter it became one of the regular episodes to be illustrated in continuous Bible histories of the twelfth and later centuries. In England it may be seen on the west front of Wells Cathedral and in the bosses of the nave of Norwich Cathedral; abroad, on the west front of Bourges, of Auxerre, at Toledo, at Orvieto—all these showing it in sculpture; while in MSS. it is very frequently to be met, and in glass—in " Creation " windows—is by no means uncommon.

NOAH

The literature attributed to Noah and his family is various. We hear of writings under his name and under those of his wife and of one of his sons.

The Book of Noah seems nowhere to be mentioned by any ancient writer; but pieces of it have been incorporated with the *Book of Enoch* and the *Book of Jubilees*. It must, therefore, be at least as old as the early part of the second century B.C.

The portions of *Enoch* which Dr. Charles (*Jubilees*, p. lxxi) describes as Noachic are chapters ii.–xi.; lx.; lxv.–lxix. 25; cvi.–cvii.; and probably xxxix. l. 2a; xli. 3–8; xliii.–xliv.; liv. 7–lv. 2; lix., but this second set has been modified.

Of these chapters, vi.–xi. contain the story of the fall of the Watchers. The most tell-tale passage is x. 1, where the Most High sends an angel (Arsalaljur, Istrael, or Uriel) " to the son of Lamech, saying, ' Go to Noah and tell him in my name,' " etc.

lx. is a vision, abruptly introduced, concerned largely with the two monsters Leviathan and Behemoth.

lxv. begins : " In those days Noah saw how the earth bowed itself," etc. In 5 the first person appears, and we read of " my grandfather Enoch." lxvii. 1, has, " The word of God came to me and spake, ' Noah, thy

lot is come up before me,' " etc.   It is mainly a prophecy
of the Flood.
  cvi., cvii. may possibly be the beginning of the Book.
They deal with the birth of Noah.   But Enoch is the
speaker.
  The second set of passages does not contain Noah's
name.
  In *Jubilees*, the Noah-passages are vii. 20–39, x. 1–15.
The former gives Noah's commandments to his sons.
At v. 26 he begins abruptly to speak in the first person :
" And we were left, I and you, my sons."
  The other (x. 1–15) tells how the demons afflicted
Noah's posterity, and how at his prayer all but a tenth
part of them were bound in the place of condemnation,
and how the angels taught Noah all the remedies for
the diseases which the demons had introduced, which
he recorded in a book and gave it to Shem.[1]   Parts of
this section exist in Hebrew in a *Book of Noah*, printed
by Jellinek and by Charles, and analyzed by Rönsch
in his *Buch der Jubiläen*.
  It will be seen that the book was of miscellaneous
character; partly legendary and haggadic, partly
apocalyptic : not unlike the *Book of Enoch*, in fact.   As
to its original compass, we have no indication whatsoever, and the absence of references to it in literature
seems to show that it went out of sight and use at an
early date.   Possibly the speeches of Noah in the
Sibylline Oracles (Book I.) may be derived from it, but
not probably; there is little that is distinctive in them.

NOAH : NORIA HIS WIFE

  Epiphanius (*Heresy*, 26) has a good deal to say about
a *Book of Noria*, the wife of Noah, which was used by
the Borborite Gnostics.   He abuses them for calling
her Noria instead of Bath Enos (which in *Jubilees*, iv. 28
is the name of Noah's mother), and relates (presumably
on the authority of the Book) that, as they say, " she

[1] There is in Syriac a book of prognostics under Shem's name
recently edited by Dr. Mingana (*Rylands Library Bulletin*).

often tried to be with Noe in the ark" (when it was being built, I understand), "and was not permitted, for the Archon who created the world wished to destroy her with all the rest in the flood; and she, they say, seated herself on the ark and set fire to it, not once or twice, but often, even a first, second, and third time. Hence the making of Noe's ark dragged on for many years, because it was so often burnt by her. For, say they, Noe was obedient to the Archon, but Noria revealed (proclaimed) the Upper Powers and Barbelo, who is of the Powers, and opposed to the Archon, like the other Powers, and taught that the elements that had been stolen from the Mother above by the Archon who made this world and the other gods, angels, and demons who were with him, should be collected from the Power that resides in bodies."

The matter about Barbelo and the Archon is, of course, Gnostic from the beginning; but it is curious to notice that in later legend Noah's wife is often referred to as trying to thwart him. A story is current in two widely separate tongues, Slavonic and English, which shows this.

Noah was enjoined to tell no man that he was making the ark; and, miraculously, his tools made no noise when he worked at it. The devil, anxious to prevent the building, went in human form to Noah's wife and asked her where her husband spent his time so secretly. She could not tell. He effectually roused her jealousy and suspicion, and gave her certain grains. "These," he said, "if put in Noah's drink, will force him to tell you all about it." This happened : Noah gave away the secret, and next day, when he went out to work, the first blow of his axe resounded through all the country-side. An angel came to him and rebuked him for his want of caution. The ark had to be finished with wattle-work.

Such is the tale as told and pictured in a beautiful fourteenth-century English MS., *Queen Mary's Prayer-book* (Brit. Mus. Royal 2. B. vii.). It is to be found also in a Newcastle mystery play, and in Slavonic

countries, whose legends are collected in Dähnhardt's
Natursagen.

The form given there (i. 258) is worth setting down,
to demonstrate the identity of the two stories. It occurs
"in a late Russian *rédaction* of the Revelations of
(Pseudo-) Methodius, with which (on this point) the
popular traditions of Russians, Poles, Hungarians,
Wotjaks, and Irtysch-Ostjaks, agree in essence."

Before the Lord şent the deluge, He commanded Noah
to build an ark secretly, and not to tell even his wife
what he was making. While Noah was at work in a
wood on a mountain, the devil came to him and asked
what he was doing, but Noah would not tell him. Then
the devil went to Noah's wife, and advised her to give
her husband an intoxicating drink, and draw the secret
from him. When Noah had taken it, his wife began
to question him, and he told her all. Next day, when
he went back to work, he found the ark all broken into
little pieces. The devil had destroyed it. Noah wept
night and day and lamented his sin. After that an angel
brought him a message of forgiveness and told him to
make the ark over again.

The trait of the noiselessness of the axe before Noah
betrayed the secret also occurs in the Hungarian story
(*l.c.* 269).

In some mystery-plays comic relief is obtained by
making Noah's wife a shrew and a scold, who will not
be induced to enter the ark until the last possible
moment.

This incident, in a more complete form, occurs in the
Russian legend just quoted. The devil asked Noah's
wife how he could get into the ark, which was now ready.
She could not think of a plan. But he told her that she
must refuse to enter the ark until the water had come
up, and must wait until Noah uttered the devil's name.
She obeyed, and however much Noah called, she would
not come, until at last he said, "Come in, you devil."
The devil immediately darted into the ark. The sequel
to this is portrayed in *Queen Mary's Prayer-book.* Noah,
on seeing the dove return, says, *Benedicite.* The devil,

unable to bear the sacred word, bursts out through the hull of the ark, but the hole he makes is stopped by the snake, who thrusts his tail into it. Many forms of this story are collected by Dähnhardt.

All this is far enough removed from the *Book of Noria*, yet the legend I have told has this much in common therewith, that it represents Noah's wife as opposed to the making of the ark under the influence of a spiritual being. Epiphanius is, as usual, confusing in his account of the transaction, but we see at least that Noria is kept away from the ark, we know not on what excuse, and we guess that she succeeds in hiding herself in it and burning it.

I conjecture that the Gnostic writer may have taken a simple folk-tale and made it a peg whereon to hang his own very uninviting bag of doctrines.

HAM

A *Prophecy of Ham* is mentioned in an obscure and unhappily defective passage of Clement of Alexandria (*Stromateis*, VI.vi. *fin.*). He is quoting the heretic Isidore, son of Basilides, and Isidore is speaking of the borrowings of Greek philosophers from Jewish Scriptures. He says : "For indeed I think that those who claim to philosophize, if they could find what is the meaning of the winged oak-tree and the embroidered mantle upon it, and all that sacred allegory that Pherecydes devised, drawing his material from the prophecy of Ham . . ." (the sentence is imperfect).

This is quite cryptic as it stands, and no great amount of light is forthcoming. In the same book (ii. 9) Clement quotes Pherecydes as saying, " Zeus makes a mantle great and fair, and on it broiders Earth and Ocean and the house of Ocean," where the words for *mantle* and *broider* are those used by Isidore. And a papyrus (Grenfell and Hunt, *Greek Papyri*, Series II, No. 11) has given us a little more of the same passage of Pherecydes ; but it does not explain the winged oak-tree.

The best opinion that is current so far about the prophecy of Ham is that of Eisler (*Weltenmantel*, etc., 1910), who connects it with the literature that went under the name of Hermes Trismegistus. The writers of that school and the alchemists who came after them (we have a good many Greek alchemical writings) professed to see a connexion between the name of Ham (Cham) and their science of Chēmeia : and Chēm figured as an interlocutor in some of the written dialogues, and is mentioned under the name of " the prophet Chymes," or " Chemes." The symbolism employed in such circles is likely to have been strange and obscure : it probably conveyed in esoteric fashion their views on cosmogony.

ABRAHAM

Of Abraham a word must be said. The lists give us the name of Abraham simply, and Nicephorus attaches to it the number of 300 lines; the MSS. also read 1300 and 3300, but 300 is best supported. The *Apostolic Constitutions* mention apocryphal writings under the names of the three patriarchs (Abraham, Isaac, Jacob); Epiphanius says that the Sethians used an *Apocalypse of Abraham* which was " full of all manner of wickedness," and Origen gives something like a quotation from an Abrahamic book, in these terms (*on Luke, Hom.* 35) : " We read—at least if any one likes to accept a writing of the kind—of the angels of righteousness and of iniquity disputing over the salvation or perdition of Abraham, each band wishing to claim him for its own company." He then refers to a passage in the *Shepherd* of Hermas. We have these Homilies on Luke only in a Latin version, and I have little doubt that the original of this passage was fuller—apocryphal quotations being apt to be slurred over, if not wholly expunged, by orthodox fourth-century translators. I also suspect that the point of the quotation has been spoilt, and that it was not Abraham's soul, but another, about whom the angels disputed.

Passing from these three references to extant literature, we find two Abraham books, one called an *Apocalypse*, the other a *Testament*, of Abraham. The *Apocalypse* exists only in Slavonic : it is accessible in a translation recently issued by the S.P.C.K., and is of considerable antiquity and great interest. The *Testament* exists in Greek, Coptic, Arabic, Ethiopic, Slavonic, Roumanian, and was edited by me in 1892.[1] All the texts of it have been more or less tampered with. The plurality of versions and revisions is in favour of the book's antiquity, and it does contain an episode which might be identified with that of Origen's quotation. 1he *Apocalypse* does not. We have seen, moreoever, that books of the Three Patriarchs are mentioned in the fourth century : and the *Testaments of Isaac and Jacob*, especially that of Isaac, have undoubtedly quite ancient elements. With them this, of Abraham, is found in Coptic, Arabic and Ethiopic.

So I think the *Testament* represents an early book, and am sure that the *Apocalypse* is early. Which of them is the text meant in the lists I will not undertake to say. They do not differ in length so much that we can decide from the stichometry.

MELCHIZEDEK

Connected with Abraham is Melchizedek. This mysterious figure interested many early thinkers, as it did the author of the *Epistle to the Hebrews*, and a sect who identified him with the Holy Spirit was either christened or christened itself Melchizedekian. Legend, both Jewish and Christian, was busy with him, identifying him sometimes with Shem, sometimes with a son of Shem, and sometimes finding other pedigrees for him. Though we do not hear from other writers of books specially concerned with him, we have two

[1] A translation of the Coptic of the *Testaments of the Three Patriarchs* is promised by Mr. Gaselee for the present series.

stories of Melchizedek which almost rank as independent apocrypha. One is in Greek, printed with the works of St. Athanasius, and setting forth that Melchizedek was the son of King Melchi and Queen Salem, and how he was converted to a belief in the true God, and at his prayer his whole kindred was swallowed up in the earth at the moment when his heathen father was about to sacrifice his other son Melchi to idols; how Melchizedek then lived as a solitary on Mount Tabor until Abraham, divinely guided, found him.

The other is a long episode attached in some MSS. to the Slavonic *Secrets of Enoch*. It will be found, in English, in Dr. Charles's edition, pp. 85–93. It is of great interest. It tells first of the succession of Mathuselam to the priesthood vacated by Enoch, then of his death and the accession of Nir, son of Lamech, and next of the miraculous birth of Melchizedek from Sopanima, wife of Nir. Melchizedek, like the mysterious Child of Rev. xii., is caught away to Paradise forty days after his birth, and thus saved from the Flood. Nir dies, and the priesthood remains vacant. A short account of Noah and the Flood ends the whole. Little attention has hitherto been paid to this story. Both it and the Greek one described above are, in their present form, Christian.

JACOB

A *Testament of Jacob*, as has been said, exists in Coptic and other Eastern languages. Besides this (which seems to be an abridged form of a longer original), something called a *Testament of Jacob* is found in a Greek MS. at Paris (Coislin, 296); but it is merely an extract from the 49th chapter of Genesis. Further, a sixteenth-century writer, Sixtus Senensis, in his *Bibliotheca Sancta*, has an entry (p. 70) worth transcribing: " There is current in print a Testament of the patriarch Jacob which Gelasius in the 29th Distinction (of the *Decretum* of Gratian) reckons among the books of apocryphal character." He here refers to the *Gelasian*

Decree, where many copies read wrongly *Testamentum Jacobi* for *Test. Jobi*. What this printed *Testament of Jacob*, current in Italy in the sixteenth century, may have been, I have not been able to determine with certainty. There is just the chance that, as the *Vision of Isaiah* was printed in Latin more than once and wholly forgotten, so some really apocryphal work may have had a brief life; but it is far more likely that some *réchauffé* of the Blessings of Jacob, circulated with the Testaments of the Twelve Patriarchs, is meant. Such a thing is, in fact, prefixed to some of the old translations of these Testaments, *e. g.* the English one printed by Richard Day.

There is, besides, a proper apocryph of Jacob in the shape of the *Ladder of Jacob*, extant only in Slavonic, and translated by Bonwetsch in the Göttingen *Nachrichten* for 1900, in two recensions. I shall reproduce this in English in the Appendix to this volume.

THE TWELVE PATRIARCHS. LEVI

The Twelve Patriarchs have their well-known *Testaments*, of which Dr. Charles has given us an indispensable edition. It seems as if behind the present Testaments there lay, in some cases, earlier documents of which we have glimpses. For instance, the story of the wars of Jacob is found in *Jubilees* and in *Jashar*, as Dr. Charles sets forth. Then, again, we have a double narrative in the *Testament of Joseph*. In that of Levi a different phenomenon occurs. A tenth-century MS. at Mount Athos (*e.* of Dr. Charles) makes two long insertions in the text: (a third, in the *Testament of Asher*, is said to be wholly Christian, and is not printed by Dr. Charles). These two passages, the first of which is not as yet translated, merit notice here.

(1) *Test. Levi II.*—" And as I kept sheep in Abel-maoul, a spirit of understanding from the Lord came upon me, and I beheld how all men had corrupted their ways and how sin was builded upon a wall (so far the ordinary text: now the Athos MS. continues):

C

"Then did I wash my garments and cleansed them in pure water, and I washed myself wholly in living water, And I made all my ways straight. Then lifted I up mine eyes and my face to heaven and opened my mouth and spake, and spread out the fingers of my hands and my hands unto truth before the holy (*plural*). And I prayed and said : Lord, thou knowest all hearts, and all the thoughts of *men's* minds thou alone perceivest [and now my children with me],[1] and give me all ways of truth. Put far from me, O Lord, the unjust spirit and *the spirit* of evil thoughts, and fornication and pride turn thou away from me. Let there be shown me, O Master, the holy spirit, and give me counsel and wisdom and knowledge and strength to do such things as please thee and to find grace in thy sight and to praise thy words. Be with me, O Lord, and let not any Satan prevail against me to make me err from thy way. And have mercy on me and bring me to thee to be thy servant and worship thee rightly : let a wall of thy peace be round about me, and a shelter of thy might cover me from all evil . . . (a corrupt word παραδωσ) : wherefore also blot out lawlessness from under heaven, put an end to lawlessness from off the face of the earth. Purify my heart, O Master, from all (un)cleanness and I will lift up (my hands) to thee; and turn not away thy face from the son of thy servant Jacob. Thou, Lord, didst bless Abraham my father and Sarah my mother, and saidst that thou wouldest give them a righteous seed, blessed for ever. Hearken also to the voice of thy servant Levi, that I may be near thee, and make me a partaker in thy words, to do true judgment for ever, even me and my sons, unto everlasting generations, and remove not the son of thy servant from before thee (from thy face) all the days of eternity. And I kept silence, though I yet prayed."

This is a corrupt and incoherent text, a cento of rather ordinary supplications without a leading thought. The vocabulary of it agrees well enough with that of

---

[1] Intrusive, or corrupt: query " And now, O Lord, bless me and my children with me," etc.

THE OLD TESTAMENT

the *Testaments*, so that it need not, and I think should
not, be regarded as a late compilation; indeed, such a
supposition is pretty well put out of court by the fact
that the second long insertion is undoubtedly antique.
The idea readily occurs to one that there may have
been Testaments of Levi, and perhaps of one or two
other leading patriarchs, a good deal longer than the
present ones, composed before the rest of the *Testaments*, and that the notion of completing the set of
twelve entailed, among other things, the compression
of existing texts.

The second insertion, part of which is also found in
Aramaic, is translated in Appendix II of Dr. Charles's
Testaments (1908, p. 228). The greater portion is put
in—quite incoherently—after *Levi* xviii. 2. The Aramaic pieces begin at an earlier point than the Greek
and carry the story on some way beyond it. A large
part of the text has to do with ritual observances, and
has much in common with *Jubilees* xxi. It has injunc-
tions given by Isaac on the authority of Abraham and
the *Book of Noah* (probably a mythical one) to Jacob
and Levi, on the ordination of the latter to be priest.
After that we have details of the birth of Levi's children,
and the text (Aramaic) ends in a paraenetic poem
addressed by Levi to his sons. Throughout he speaks
in the first person. Dr. Charles regards this fragment
as an original source both of the *Testaments* and of
Jubilees, in which case it would have to be as old as
the third century B.C.

THE PRAYER OF JOSEPH

And now we come to the consideration of a very
interesting lost book, the *Prayer of Joseph*. The lists
have told us that it contained 1100 lines—as many as
are assigned to *Wisdom ;* and we have certain fragments
of it preserved by Origen, which must be transcribed
and expounded in detail.

The first and longest is in Origen's *Commentary
upon John*, ii. 31.

He is speaking of John the Baptist, and, says he :
" It will not be out of place to add a notion of our own
about him. When we read the prophecy of him,
' Behold, I send my angel before thy face,' etc., we
reflected if by chance one of the holy angels being
upon service were not sent down as a forerunner of
our Saviour. It would not, indeed, be surprising if,
when the firstborn of all creation became incarnate,
for love of man, some should have become emulators
and imitators of Christ, and embraced the opportunity
of ministering to His kindness to men by means of a
like body. . . . Now if any one accepts among the
apocrypha current among the Hebrews, what is entitled
the *Prayer of Joseph*, he will derive from it exactly this
teaching, expressed in plain terms : that those who
from the beginning possessed some special *excellence*
beyond men, and were greatly superior to all other
souls, have descended from the estate of angels into
human nature. Jacob, at any rate, says : ' For I
Jacob that speak unto you, I am also Israel, an
angel of God and a ruling spirit, and Abraham and
Isaac were pre-created ($\pi\rho o\epsilon\kappa\tau i\sigma\theta\eta\sigma a\nu$, a word only
found here) before any work. And I Jacob, that am
called by men Jacob, yet my name is Israel, that am
called by God Israel, a man seeing God, for I am the
first begotten of every living thing that is quickened
by God.' " And he continues : " And I, when I was
coming from Mesopotamia of Syria, Uriel the angel of
God came forth and said that I had come down (came)
to earth and tabernacled among men, and that I was
called by name Jacob. He envied me and fought with
me, and wrestled with me, saying that his name should
have precedence of my name and of the angel that is
before all (*or* that his name and the name of the angel
that is before all should have precedence of my name).
(*All* is singular, and should perhaps be rendered ' before
every (angel).') And I told him his name, and in what
order [1] he is among the sons of God, *saying :* ' Art not
thou Uriel, the eighth from me, and I am Israel, an

---

[1] Edd. $\pi\acute{o}\sigma o s$, but $\pi\acute{o}\sigma\tau o s$ (*quotus*) is certainly to be read.

archangel of the power of the Lord, and a captain of
captains of thousands among the sons of God? Am I
not Israel, the first minister before the face of God?'
And I called upon my God by the inextinguishable
name." "It is likely" (Origen goes on) "that if these
words were really spoken by Jacob, and therefore recorded, that the incident 'He supplanted his brother
in the womb' (Hos. xii. 3) happened intelligently (con-
sciously, συνετῶσ)." He then speaks a little about
Jacob and Esau, hinting at their possible pre-existence,
and concludes : "But we have made a considerable
digression in taking up the matter of Jacob and calling
in as evidence a writing not lightly to be despised, to
make something more credible of the theory about
John, which maintains that he, according to Isaiah's
word, being an angel, took a body in order to bear
witness to the Light." This passage is summarized
by Jerome *on Haggai.*

The second fragment is in the *Philocalia,* cap. xxiii.
15, taken from the *Commentary on Genesis* iii. It is
partly to be found in Eusebius' *Præp. Evang.,* VI. 11,
and Procopius *on Genesis* quotes from it too. The topic
is astrology.

"For, as we showed before that the fact that God
knows what every man will do is no obstacle to freewill, so neither do the signs which God has appointed
for the giving of information impede freewill : but, like
a book containing future events in prophecy, the whole
heaven—the book of God, as it is—may contain the
future. Wherefore in the *Prayer of Joseph* this word
of Jacob may be thus understood : 'For I have read
in the tablets of heaven all that shall befall you and
your sons.'

(19) "But if Jacob says he has read in the tablets of
heaven what is to befall his sons, and upon this point
some one objects to us that the opposite of what we
have said is shown by the Scripture (for we were saying
that man has no apprehension of the signs, whereas
Jacob says he has read in the tablets of heaven), we shall
say in defence that our wise men, aided by a spirit

excelling human nature, are taught secret things not humanly but divinely, as Paul, who says, 'I heard unspeakable words,' etc. . . . And, besides, Jacob was greater than man, he who supplanted his brother, and who declares in that same book from which we quoted, 'I read in the tablets of heaven' that he was a captain of captains of thousands of the power (host) of the Lord, and had of old the name of Israel : which *fact* he recognizes while doing service in a body, being reminded of it by the archangel Uriel."

The next allusion is in the *Annals* of Michael Glycas, a Byzantine chronicler of the twelfth century. He has given a *résumé* of the story of Tobit, and when he comes to the name of the archangel Raphael, he says, "And this name Raphael thou hast already learnt out of Tobit, but that of Uriel, as the great Psellus (Michael Psellus, 1081) says, neither the Old nor the New Testament makes known to us. But there is a Hebraic book, unknown to most men, entitled the *Prayer of Joseph*, where his father Jacob is introduced as talking with this angel [Raphael]; though now the book, like the other apocryphal writings, is rejected and set at nought by the Hebrews." The bracketed name of Raphael must be wrong. The reference to Psellus, much of whose writing remains inedited, has never been followed up. Very likely he depended upon Origen for his knowledge of the *Prayer*.

In the *Ascension of Isaiah*, iv. 22, a number of prophetic writings are mentioned : the twelve minor prophets are enumerated, and then "the words of Joseph the Just, and the words of Daniel." Here it is generally assumed that the *Prayer of Joseph* is meant. The passage has been thought to be an addition to the *Ascension :* at latest it would be of the third century, at earliest late in the first.

In the *Revue Bénédictine* Dom Morin has an article on the library of the Abbey of Gorze in the eleventh century. To it he appends a note upon a collection of Latin homilies attributed to a certain John, which he had seen in MSS. then extant at Reims and at Arras.

(Are they still in being?) " I noticed," he says, " a mention of the angel Uriel; on p. 62 are the words, Et pugnavit cum angelo Oriel (and he fought with the angel Uriel)." I do not see that this can refer to any one but Jacob, and it is not independent of the *Prayer of Joseph*. It is quite likely, of course, to have been derived from Origen, who, when all is said, remains our sole source of knowledge of the contents of the book.

A very lengthy comment might be written upon these fragments. I will try to compress mine.

First, the title, *Prayer of Joseph*, is peculiar. No other separate book is so named, though a good many prayers occurring in Scriptural books are dignified with special titles, and some were current separately. Such are the Prayers of Moses (Ps. xc.), of Habakkuk, of Solomon in *Kings*, and in *Wisdom*, of Jesus son of Sirach (Ecclus. li.), of Azarias in the furnace (Dan. iii. (LXX)), of Esdras (4 Esdr. viii), of Baruch (*Apoc. Baruch*), of Manasseh. But these are not whole books. The nearest parallel is the case of the *Book* or *History of Asenath*, which the Armenian list places in the stead of the Joseph book, and calls the *Prayer* (prayers) *of Asenath*. A Greek MS. of it has a similar title, *Confession and Prayer of Asenath*. The fact that Asenath replaces Joseph suggests the possibility of an integral connexion between the books (so Mgr. Batiffol). I have tried to establish one, but with little success. The most one can say is that in *Asenath* a sort of divinity hangs about both Jacob and Joseph : that Levi " saw writings written in the heavens," that the angel who visits Asenath is " captain of the host of the Lord God, leader of all the army of the Most High." He has a name " written in heaven in the book of the Most High by the finger of God, before all. And the things written in that book are ineffable, such as men may not speak or hear." Joseph is described as the son of the Most High. The description of Jacob says that his arms were as those of an angel, his thighs and legs and feet like a giant's, and he like a man that fought (*or* might fight) with God. I think it quite probable that the writer of this was acquainted with the *Prayer of Joseph ;* but I do not see (as I should like to see) evidence that the one book has drawn much from the other or is modelled upon it.

All that we can fairly gather from the title is that the book must have contained a prayer or prayers of considerable bulk uttered by Joseph (as *Asenath* contains a long prayer of Asenath). On what occasion it was offered, whether in the pit, or in prison, or on his deathbed, there is no certainty.

From the fragments we can gather one point of importance. Jacob says, "I that speak unto *you*, I have read what shall befall *you* and your sons." He is therefore addressing some or all of his descendants, and he does so in the terms used by the Patriarchs in the *Testaments* when they are on their deathbeds. Also, I think, the revelation of his angelic nature is one which would naturally be reserved until the end of his life. Further, in Gen. xlviii., where the blessing of Joseph's sons is related, there are coincidences of expression : " My God," and " When I was coming from Mesopotamia of Syria." Thus the book contained a dying speech of Jacob, of which we have a portion. I am tempted to think that it was addressed to Joseph and his sons Ephraim and Manasseh. The grounds are naturally slight : (*a*) We already have, in Genesis xlix., the full address of Jacob to the twelve; (*b*) there are coincidences of language with the episode of Joseph's sons in Gen. xlviii.

The matter and doctrine of the fragments occupy us next. The pre-existence of Jacob as an angel, and of Abraham and Isaac is here taught in the crudest way. The terms, however, are confusing. If Jacob is first-begotten of every living thing, is he senior to Abraham and Isaac? One must doubt whether the writer had thought this out. He is bent on emphasizing the dignity of Jacob, and finds himself forced to mention the two other Patriarchs.

On pre-existence of souls in general a good deal has been written : an essay by F. C. Porter in *O. T. and*

Semitic Studies in Memory of President Harper, is a notable contribution to the subject. His thesis is that the Jewish doctrine of the pre-existence of ordinary human souls does not imply a belief in a full personal existence of them. We, however, are concerned with the personal pre-existence of certain individuals. Rabbinic literature has a little light to throw on this. The *Midrash Rabba*, I. § 4, gives (as do other books) a list of things that were created before the world. The Torah and the Throne of Glory (Prov. viii. 22, Ps. xciii. 2) : these were created already; four more came into God's mind to be created : the Patriarchs (Hos. ix. 10 : I saw your fathers as the first-ripe in the fig-tree at her first time), Israel (Ps. lxxiv. 2), the Sanctuary (Jer. xvii. 12), the name of Messiah (Ps. lxxii. 17). Sometimes Repentance is added. We find the list also in *Midrash Tanchuma* and the *Pirke R. Eliezer* (where the phrase is " the spirits of the fathers "). It does not quite come up to our text in precision of statement. Older books can be cited. *Enoch* xlviii. 3, says of the Son of Man, " Before the sun and moon and the signs were created, before the stars of heaven were made, his name was named before the Lord of Spirits." Moses (*Assumption*, i. 14) says of himself, " God foresaw (*not* created) me before the foundation of the world that I should be the mediator of his covenant."

Ideas about pre-existence were in the air, and it is even possible that the words of Christ in John viii. 58, " Before Abraham was, I am," are to be regarded as showing a consciousness, and containing a contradiction, of such beliefs.

As to the phrase " first-begotten of every living thing," one O.T. text may be cited as a parallel, Exod. iv. 22, " Israel is my firstborn son "; but far nearer is St. Paul's phrase in Col. i. 15, " the firstborn of every creature."

In the *Shepherd* of Hermas, *Vision* III. 2, 5, we read of the (seven) holy angels who were first created. Clement of Alexandria mentions them rather frequently, *e. g.* in *Str.* VI. 143 : " Seven are they that

have the greatest power, the first begotten rulers of
the angels." We also find them in the *Pirke R. Eliezer*,
4 : " The seven angels that were first created."
" That his name should have precedence over my
name and over that of the angel before every . . ."
Schürer would read, " and before every angel" (πρὸ τοῦ
παντὸσ ἀγγέλου for τοῦ πρὸ παντὸσ ἀγγέλου), but I do not
think the text can be mended so easily. It depends
on one sole MS., and I fear it is defective. More important is it to notice another Pauline parallel : " He
hath given him a name which is above every name,"
etc. No Jewish Scripture supplies a better.

Uriel is the wrestling angel. This, again, is peculiar.
The uniform Rabbinic tradition says that it was Michael,
Pseudo-Philo (*Bibl. Antiq.*, XVIII 6) that it was the
angel who is over the praises, the *Ladder of Jacob* that
it was the archangel Sarekl : in *Pirke R. Eliezer* the
wrestling angel gives his own name Israel to Jacob. I
do not trace the reason for choosing Uriel. He figures
a good deal in *Enoch :* in xx. 2 he is the angel over the
world and over Tartarus; he guides Enoch to remote
regions and shows him the movements of the heavenly
bodies. He is one of the four great angels, Michael,
Gabriel, and Raphael being his compeers. To Adam
he comes as the angel over repentance and tells him of
the hours of day and night. To Esdras he shows
visions. In the *Apocalypse of Peter* (and *Sib. Orac.* II)
he brings souls out of Hades to judgment. In the
Testament of Solomon we read of a demon who was an
offspring of Uriel, and Uriel is summoned to control
him.

He appears in our fragment in a somewhat unfavour-
able light, seeming to take advantage of Jacob's (Israel's)
confinement in a human body to gain a superiority
over him, which he (no doubt) hopes to maintain when
Jacob's earthly life is over.

Of the phrases " come down to earth " and " tabernacled among men," the second is paralleled by
Baruch iii. 38, Rev. xxi. 3, and especially Ecclus. xxiv.
8–10 : the first has its closest illustration in Eph. iv. 9–10.

"Uriel the eighth from me." Another contradiction of tradition. Israel appears here as the first of a band of seven, all of whom were before Uriel. Uriel is elsewhere always one of the first seven, and usually of the first four. The place here claimed by Jacob-Israel is that assigned by almost universal consent to Michael.

"And I called on my God by the inextinguishable name." Does this begin a fresh sentence and mean that after thus addressing Uriel, Jacob called upon God? or is it to be connected with the last clause, meaning that, in the discharge of his functions in heaven, Israel invoked Him? In this latter case the greatness of the Name would be the important point, and the intention would be to show how exalted was Jacob's ministry. In spite of the fact that the verb is in the aorist and not in the imperfect, I incline to the latter interpretation. The expression "inextinguishable name" I have not as yet found elsewhere, though I believe it to exist.

These are the chief points in the first fragment. The second is: "I read in the tablets of heaven all that shall befall you and your sons."

The tablets of heaven figure in three books, *Enoch* (four times) *Jubilees* (over twenty times), the *Testaments of the Twelve Patriarchs* (thrice).

The *Enoch* passages are lxxxi. 1, 2 (the book of the deeds of all men . . . to the remotest generations), xciii. 2 (they contain the destinies of the righteous), ciii. 2 (the reward of the righteous), cvi. 19, cvii. 1 (generation after generation will transgress).

In *Jubilees*, iii. 10, the laws of the purification of women are written in the heavenly tablets, and in sixteen other passages decrees or legal enactments are registered in them. In three cases events are recorded as they happen, and in two others, future matters. But to us the really important passage is xxxii. 21 ff. Jacob at Bethel (not on his flight in Gen. xxviii., but later in his life) "saw in a vision of the night, and behold an angel descended from heaven with seven tablets in his hands, and he gave them to Jacob, and he read them

and knew all that was written therein which would
befall him and his sons throughout all the ages."

In the *Testaments*, *Levi* (v.) speaks of the slaughter
of Shechem as written on the tablets (as *Jubilees* xxx.
19, 20), *Asher* (ii.) says that the distinction between
clean and unclean is declared there (also in the manner
of *Jubilees*); and in vii. 5, " I have read (*or* known) in
the tablets of the heavens that ye will surely be dis-
obedient," etc. In each of these cases Dr. Charles
eliminates the phrase "tablets of the heavens" for
reasons which seem to me unsound. In each case
there is a distinct resemblance to the use of the phrase
in *Jubilees*.

We cannot be wrong, I think, in connecting the
phrase in the *Prayer of Joseph* with the passage in
Jubilees xxxi., and in supposing that in the *Prayer* the
same vision of Jacob at Bethel is referred to.

The leading idea of the principal fragment is that
angels can become incarnate in human bodies, live on
earth in the likeness of men, and be unconscious of
their original state. Israel does so apparently in order
that he may become the father of the chosen people.
It is, I believe, a doctrine which is unique in Jewish
teaching.

It has been held—*e. g.* by J. T. Marshall (Hastings'
Dict. Bible, II. 778)—that the *Prayer* was definitely anti-
Christian : it claimed for the Patriarchs the same
sublime and supernatural characteristics as Christians
claimed for Our Lord. Also, whereas in early Christian
exegesis the wrestling angel is identified with the Logos,
the pre-existent Christ (as by Justin and Origen), the
status of that angel is here lowered in favour of Israel.
These are substantial arguments. I would add that
the fragments appear to show knowledge of Christian
ideas and terminology. These are the points : (*a*) pre-
existence of the Patriarchs as opposed to "Before
Abraham was, I am"; (*b*) incarnation; (*c*) firstborn of
every living thing; (*d*) "his name should have precedence of mine."

Upon the whole I incline to think that the author of

the *Prayer of Joseph* knew something of Christian theology and indulged in some side-hits at it. Whether that was the main object of the book we cannot tell; but Origen treats it with such respect that I think its attack on Christianity cannot have been very overt.

In the *Journal of Theological Studies*, xx. (1918) p. 20, Mr. Vacher Burch advocates the view that the *Prayer* was pro-Christian, and based on the primitive *Testimonia* against the Jews. " The chief theme of the fragments . . . is the surpassing of one angel-appearance of the Christ by another—of Uriel by Israel." It is now known that Uriel was a Testimony hypostasis of this nature, for the Ethiopic *Narrative of St. Clement* (Budge, *Contendings of the Apostles*, ii. 479) contains this helpful passage : " And I (Peter) gave them commandments concerning circumcision according to the Law of Moses, and God (*i. e.* Christ) appeared unto me in the form of the Angel Uriel, and commanded me to do away the Old Law and to bring in the New." He refers also to the fact that Justin Martyr makes Jacob and Israel names of Christ. I cannot reproduce the whole of the passage here : the thesis is to me unconvincing at present. It is obscurely put by Mr. Burch, and needs restatement in an expanded form to make it plausible, or indeed intelligible. See further under *Hezekiah*.

JANNES AND MAMBRES

Jannes and Jambres (or Mambres). The *Penitence of Jannes and Mambres* is mentioned in the *Gelasian Decree*. Origen (*on Matthew* xxv.) says : " Paul's statement, ' As Jannes and Mambres withstood Moses ' (2 Tim. iii. 8) is not found in the ' public ' scriptures, but in a secret (apocryphal) book entitled the Book of Jannes and Mambres." The writer called Ambrosiaster, *on 2 Timothy*, says : " This example is from the Apocrypha. For Jannes and Mambres were brothers, magicians or poisoners, of the Egyptians, who thought they could resist by the art of their magic the mighty works of God which were being accomplished through them. But when the might of Moses in his works proved greater, they were humbled, and confessed, with the pain of their wounds (cf. Philostorgius, below), that it was God that wrought in Moses."

These are the old allusions that imply the existence of a book of Jannes and Mambres. There is a good deal of scattered legend about them, chiefly Jewish. They are the two sons of Balaam (Num. xxi. 22) : they educated Moses (Abulpharaj) : they were drowned in the Red Sea, or slain with their father by Phinehas. St. Macarius visited their tomb, which was full of demons, from whom he obtained leave to enter and look round. He found a brazen vessel hanging by an iron chain in a well and much consumed by time, and also a number of dried-up pomegranates (Palladius, *Hist. Lausiaca*).

Another set of allusions is in heathen writers. Numenius, quoted by Eusebius, names them, and so does Artapanus. Pliny speaks confusedly (*N. H.*, xxx. 11) of the magicians Moses, Jannes, Jotapa; and Apuleius (*Apology*, 90), enumerating famous wizards, names Jesus perhaps, and certainly Moses and Jannes, Apollonius, Dardanus, Zoroaster, Hostanes.

The allusions to the two wizards which occur in Oriental chronicles have been collected by Iselin in *Zeitschrift f. Wissenschaftl. Theol.*, 1894, 321.

We now come to consider possible fragments of the book. Photius's excerpts from Philostorgius's *Ecclesiastical History* has one (ix. 2, p. 166, ed. Bidez) : " Moses chastised Jannes and Jambres with sores and sent the mother of one of them to death." This must have been introduced by Philostorgius as an illustration : the ninth book of the *History* is concerned with the reign of Valens.

In the eleventh-century MS. Cotton Tiberius B. V , appended to a tract *On the Marvels of the East*, is the following fragment in Latin and Anglo-Saxon, illustrated by a beautiful picture of Mambres doing an incantation, and hell open with souls in it.

" Mambres opened the magical books of his brother Jannes, and did necromancy and brought up from hell the shade of his brother. The soul of Jannes answered him saying : I thy brother died not unjustly, but of a truth justly, and judgment will go against me, for I was wiser than all wise magicians, and I withstood the two brethren, Moses and Aaron, who did great signs and wonders : therefore died I and was brought down from among *men* into hell, where there is great burning, and the pit (lake) of perdition, whence there is no coming up. And now, my brother Mambres, take heed to thyself in thy lifetime to do good to thy sons and thy friends : for in hell there is nothing of good, but sadness and darkness : and when thou shalt have died and shalt be in hell among the dead, thy dwelling-place and thy abode (seat) will be twenty (*probably* two) cubits broad and four cubits long."

With the *Penitence of Jannes and Mambres* in the *Gelasian Decree* is classed the *Penitence of Cyprian* (the magician and martyr of Antioch, the parent of the Faust-legend). This we have, and it gives an account of his initiation into the devil's service. There are two mentions of our wizards in it : § 6. The prince of the devils praises Cyprian, and calls him a youth of good gifts, a new Jambres, apt for the ministry. § 17. Cyprian says of himself : " I do not believe there was ever a worse man than I was : I outdid the Jannes and Jambres of history. They in the midst of their lying wonders acknowledged the finger of God, but I was wholly set upon it that there was no God. If God did not pardon them who even partly recognized Him, how should He pardon me who ignored Him altogether? " In this view the Egyptian magicians, it seems, did not find forgiveness.

The Greek *Acts of St. Katherine* are printed in three texts by J. Viteau (Paris, 1897). The first says that Katherine had studied all the art of Hippocrates, Galen, Aristotle, Homer, Plato, Philistion, Eusebius, and the necromancies of Jannes and Jambres and the Sibyl. The second repeats this, more than once, and also gives two quotations from Jannes and Mambres, the first of which defies translation, but adds : " They show, to them that seek to behold, the faces (*or* persons) that have slept in the earth from the ages." The other is better : " But concerning the mountains (*sic*—? mules) Jannes and Jambres spake, signifying the sign of the manger of the Lord; and concerning the stone whereby the stone of the tomb (*a verb is wanted*), as also it was said by the prophet : The stone which the builders rejected," etc.

If this is a genuine quotation at all (and one from the Sibyl which precedes it is correct) it implies Messianic, even Christian, predictions in the book.

Philostorgius by speaking of the mother " of one of them " (θατέρου) contradicts the tradition that the two men were brothers, if he is to be taken literally.

The Latin fragment remains the best. It would form a possible opening for the book, or it might come near the end of it : it would hardly be the closing note. Mambres must have made some reply, and even perhaps repented as a *finale*. But we must confess ourselves quite ignorant of the general character of the *Penitence*. It was older, we see, than Origen, and it may have been Christian. Cyprian's *Penitence* is possibly modelled upon it to some extent.

By way of appendix a curious fragment may find a place here. In the Roman edition of the works of Ephraem Syrus (ii. p. 405), in the midst of the Syriac *Testament of Ephraem* is suddenly interpolated the following piece of Syriac verse, which has no link of connexion with its context, and which I here translate from the Latin rendering :

" In the time of Moses the magicians rose up against the son of Amram : but the finger of God overcame them, as they themselves also confessed.

" The righteousness of God smote the wicked men with an evil sore, that even against their will they might proclaim the truth : for the Truth is wont to bear patiently until deceivers repent : but when they are puffed up and think themselves safe, then are they cast down into the pit.

" For when Moses was sent to bring the people out of

Egypt, at the bidding of Pharaoh's Lord he came to Pharaoh and told him the command of God. When Pharaoh heard it he was driven to rage and fury and turned to blasphemy; and when the matter was published throughout the city and was come to the ears of the nobles of those parts, some said : It is the command of God and must be obeyed at all costs.

" But the King, when he saw Moses, feared, and began to feel the punishment that hung over him.

" Is there any that does not fear at the sight of the Lord? or who would not tremble at beholding God? So Pharaoh feared Moses, because he was the god of Pharaoh.

" The whole multitude of the magicians of Egypt hasted together to see a new marvel, for in the face of Moses was the angel of fire and wind, surpassing the brightness of the sun and of lightning, so that whoever fixed his eyes on him took him for a god; but they who heard his voice—for he was stammering and stuttered—despised and contemned him as a man. And one affirmed that he was come down from heaven : another set him wholly at naught : for, said he, if there were any great thing *in him*, surely he would have healed himself.

" Now Moses, as you have heard, knew the tongue of that country well; bred up in the house of Pharaoh, he had drunk in all the wisdom of the Egyptians, as the Apostle witnesses to us of him. And though he were not aware of it himself, yet he had the Holy Spirit dwelling in him, from whom he had learned all that had happened from Adam even to his own days, and was not ignorant of what the magicians were plotting against him.

" So Pharaoh called together all the magicians and their disciples and spoke to them of Moses thus : It is now time that whatever power you have you should put forth for the common good. When war is upon us there is need of mighty men, and the skill of physicians appears then when diseases are rife. Throughout all the world the people will laugh at us with great disgrace

D

of our name if we are overcome by this stammering
stutterer. Be therefore strong in conflict till we bear
off victory : contend valiantly till we triumph. There
is no man who knows not our name or extols you not
.as workers of wonders : we (ye?) have been wont to be
helpers even of Kings when war came upon them.
If then they see us made a laughing-stock to a stammerer,
much more shall we be despised by all other men. Up
then, put on a manly spirit, and go forth to battle like
heroes of renown, that we may gain an eternal name;
and so all who hear of it may be smitten with fear and
not dare to resist our people. And though I excel in
royal dignity, yet I uphold the common cause with you.
To all of us there will be like honour or like shame.

"The magicians, stirred by these words, as if made
drunk with wine, promised seas and mountains to
Pharaoh King of Egypt. The sun, said they, shall not
again rise to lighten Egypt before the son of Amram has
ceased to live. What time thou, O King, takest quiet
slumber in thy bed, then shalt thou hear that Moses
has been punished by a shameful death. And this,
indeed, we account as nothing : it is child's play. Come
then, enter thy chamber and climb up upon thy bed
and sleep : for the death of Moses is at the doors, and he
shall not, believe us, see another day.

"Thus the magicians left Pharaoh. And he, believing
their words, could not sleep for his impatience, looking
for the dawn of day : nor, had he slept, could he rest
without the coming of the same images to him in his
slumber.

"But they, practising their arts, called up devils
and sent them against Moses. The evil spirits rushed
in hosts upon the holy man : but the power of God and
the prayer of the righteous one drove them back as the
storm scatters the fire and the wind the smoke. So
did the demons fly from the face of Moses as the conquered flee in battle before the victors, and thieves turn
their backs when they hear the voices of the watchmen
approaching.

"As light dispels darkness, so did Moses drive away

the wicked ones. Headlong they returned to the magicians by whom they had been hired; and, said they : We lose our labour against this man, for he is stronger than we, and we cannot get near to the border of the place where he dwells.

" Meanwhile the day dawned, and Pharaoh anxiously expected that what the magicians had promised him, of the death of Moses, should have been fulfilled. But when the appointed time was past, and there came none to tell the tidings he desired, the King called the magicians and spake thus to them : Why, said he, hath the matter fallen out otherwise than as you promised ? for you said, Moses shall not see another day after this.

" The magicians said to him : Have patience a little : the man's death is indeed near, but we can do nothing in haste, O King, and this day allows it not, for to-day it is new moon : when the moon begins to wane, then shall the life of Moses fail.

" This was the cause they pretended to him, until the appointed hour should come to Moses : but the King received their words gladly, being subject to the same errors as they.

" The magicians therefore set to work : they took somewhat of the hairs and garments of Moses, and made an image of him, and laid it up in a tomb, and set evil demons against it. Immediately the demons came, and the princes of them : Satan was ready with his hosts, all of them in divers forms, to destroy Moses.

" They ran against him in a troop. But when they lifted up their eyes to the holy prophet and saw him encompassed by a host of angels, like as it was once with Elisha, they could not bear the look of him, much less attack him, and all together they fled away in confusion with cries and howlings.

" This thing brought the magicians to perplexity. They turned therefore to other means to save their name and not be found guilty of deceit and lying before the King. Accordingly they took a cup full of wine and by their enchantments compelled vipers and dragons to spue their venom into it ; and when it was ready they

gave the cup to Moses, that he might drink it and burst
asunder. Take, said they, this wine which the King
of Egypt sends thee, and drink it, for to this pinnacle
of honour he will have thee raised, as he hath long ago
desired; and this wine itself is like the desire of the
King, for it is old, and by reason of length of time is
become muddy and dark.

" At this Moses smiled, and took the cup and signed
it in the name of God and drank the wine without any
hurt. But that they might know that their deceit
was not hidden from him, he turned to them and said :
Come, tell the King, who hath sent me to drink wine
mingled with the poison of serpents, that none of these
things do any hurt to the servants of God.

" Thus far concerning Moses and the Magicians."

The elegancies of the poetic form are not so excessive
as to disguise the story, and it is one which I do not
find elsewhere. The drinking of the poison is like, or
has been made like, the famous miracle of St. John the
Evangelist : the " signing " of the cup may well be a
touch of the poet's; it is the only one that is obviously
Christian. I should not be at all surprised to find that
we had here a paraphrase of part of the story of Jannes
and Mambres. Note that the unsuccessful attacks of
the demons are just such as occur in the *Penitence of
Cyprian*, which is linked with that of the Egyptian
wizards. The (Latin) *Acts* of St. James the Great
contain something similar, in the tale of Hermogenes
and Philetus.

ELDAD AND MEDAD

Eldad and Medad (Modat) was a short book of 400 lines,
longer than Ephesians (312), shorter than 2 Corinthians
(590). Of it we have one certain fragment. Hermas,
who in the *Shepherd* makes many unacknowledged
borrowings, quotes a scripture by name once and once
only. In *Vision* ii. 5 he says : " The Lord is near unto
them that turn to Him, as it is written in Eldad and
Medad, who prophesied to the people in the wilderness."

We cannot doubt that the matter of the book was the

prophetic utterances of Eldad and Medad. Legend has not been very busy with their names, but the Midrashim (*Tanchuma*) and Targums say something of them and of what they prophesied. They are made half-brothers of Moses, in two ways. (1) According to the author of the *Hebrew Questions on Chronicles* (iv. 17), attributed to Jerome, they had other names, Epher and Jalon. After the giving of the Law, he goes on, Moses commanded his father Amram to put away his wife Jochebed, because she, being Levi's daughter, was aunt to her husband. Amram did so, married again, and Eldad and Medad were his offspring. (2) A Midrash says that after Amram's death Jochebed married Elizaphan and bore Eldad and Medad to him. The gift of prophecy was bestowed on them (*Sanhedrin*, 1) because when chosen among the seventy Elders they said they were unworthy of the honour. *Tanchuma* says they prophesied of things that were to happen as long as forty years after, whereas the other Elders only predicted things near at hand. Alone among the Elders their names are recorded; they kept their gift of prophecy and entered the Promised Land. They prophesied of the death of Moses and succession of Joshua (so also Pseudo-Philo); or, say others, of the quails; or of Gog and Magog.

We have seen that Hermas at Rome quotes *Eldad and Medad*. In Clement of Rome's letter, and in the Homily that is called his second Epistle, a prophetical passage is quoted without a name, which Bishop Lightfoot guessed to be taken from this same book. The guess is an interesting one, and the passage shall be given here. There are considerable differences between the two quotations.

I. Clem., 23; II. 11 : " Far be from you that scripture where it saith (for the prophetic word also saith, II.) : Miserable are the double-minded which doubt in their soul (heart, II.), which say : (all, II.) these things we heard in our fathers' days also, and lo ! we have grown old and nothing of these things hath befallen us (but we expecting from day to day have seen none of these

things, II.). O foolish ones, compare yourselves to a
tree; take the vine; first it sheddeth the leaf, then a
shoot cometh (then a leaf, then a flower : II.
omits), and after that a sour berry, then a cluster fully ripe.
(Here I. ends; II. continues) : So also my people hath
had unquietnesses and afflictions : afterward it shall
receive good things."
The resemblance to 2 Peter iii. 4, etc. (where is the
promise of his coming?) is pointed out· by Lightfoot.
The difficulty I find in acquiescing in Lightfoot's
conjecture is that I do not quite see whom Eldad and
Medad would be addressing. In the story as we have
it in Numbers xi., their prophecy is uttered not very
long after the giving of the Law, and just before the
gift of the quails. The people have not been long in
the wilderness—not long enough, it seems to me, to make
it appropriate that they should say " we have grown old
in looking for the fulfilment of the promises." Such
language would be more fitting in the mouth of Israel
when in exile and hoping for the Return. And so I
think that those are perhaps more likely to be right who
suggest that the apocryphal Ezekiel is the source of
this passage.

OG

*The Book of Og the Giant, who is said by the heretics to
have fought with a dragon after the Flood.* This is the
most sensational entry in the Gelasian Decree. How
we should like to have the book in which such stirring
incidents were related !
What can we elicit from records, or reasonably conjecture, about it ? It was circulated by heretics. What
heretics? I guess the Manichæans, for in a list of
Manichæan books given by Timotheus, Presbyter of
Constantinople (Fabricius, *Cod. Apocr. N.T.*, i. 139)
is one called " The matter (or treatise) of the Giants "
(ἡ τῶν γιγάντων πραγματεία), which may fairly be
identified with the *Book of Og.* Other Manichæan
writings—the *Foundation* and the *Treasure of Life*—

are condemned, be it noted in passing, in the Gelasian Decree.

But how should Og, who was conquered and slain by Moses, have fought with a dragon after the Flood? It is the constant Rabbinic story that he was one of the antediluvian giants, and that he escaped the Flood by riding on the roof of Noah's ark, being fed by Noah : and, further, that he was identical with Eliezer the servant of Abraham. Once one of his teeth fell out, and Abraham made an armchair out of it. This and many other stories demonstrating his great size, may be found collected in Eisenmenger's *Entdecktes Judenthum*, or Baring Gould's *Legends of Old Testament Characters*. But there is nothing in them about a dragon.

An unexpected source gives what may be a reminiscence of that incident. In the metrical Anglo-Saxon *Dialogue of Salomon and· Saturn* are the following question and answer :—

" *Salomon :* Tell me of the land where no man may step with feet.

" *Saturnus* quoth : The sailor over the sea, the noble one, ·was named Wandering Wolf (weallende Wulf), well known unto the tribes of the Philistines, the friend of Nebrond (= Nimrod). He slew upon the plain five-and twenty dragons at daybreak, and himself fell down there dead : therefore that·land may not any man—that boundary place any one visit, nor bird fly over it, or any more the cattle of the field. Thence the poisonous race first of all widely arose, which now bubbling through breath of poison force their way. Yet shines his sword mightily sheathed, and over his burial-place glimmer the hilts."

Only a reminiscence, clearly,. if that : for Og, we see, survived the combat for many centuries. But quite possibly a reminiscence, for the hero is of the right sort of date, the friend of Nimrod, and early enough to be connected with the rise of the whole tribe of venomous beasts.

Dragons and floods are not unconnected in mythology. Sometimes the dragon, it is thought, is a torrent or flood personified; sometimes (as in Rev. xii. 15) he is the source of it. We may remember that it was after the Deucalion flood that the Python took up his abode at Delphi, where Apollo slew him. Some such myth as that lies, perhaps, at the bottom of the lost story of Og.

MOSES (APOCALYPSE, TESTAMENT, ASSUMPTION)

To *Moses* two entries are devoted in the lists. We have the *Testament*, 1100 lines long, and the *Assumption*, 1400. Besides that, an *Apocalypse of Moses* is named; George the Syncellus says that Gal. v. 6; vi. 15 (In Christ Jesus neither circumcision availeth anything, etc.) is from the *Apocalypse of Moses :* a marginal *scholium* in several MSS. of the Epistles agrees that it is " from an apocryphon of Moses." There must be some mistake. The only text in Galatians which could be plausibly assigned to such a source is iii. 19 : " It was ordained by angels in the hand of a mediator," which might be an allusion to the *Assumption* (God foresaw me . . . to be the mediator of His covenant) : no conceivable Jewish book could have contained the statement of Gal. v. 6, and no Christian forger of early times ever did his work quite so badly. At some ancient date the marginal reference must have been attached to the wrong place, and our authorities have copied it in its dislocated state. (A passage which might more plausibly be referred to a book called the *Apocalypse of Moses* is 2 Cor. xi. 14 (Satan is transformed into an angel of light), for this does happen in the *Life of Adam :* and the Greek recension of that is called the *Apocalypse of Moses*.)

Two *Apocalypses of Moses* we have : the name is an alternative title of the *Book of Jubilees*, according to George Cedrenus; and there is a Greek *Apocalypse of Moses* (ed. Tischendorf, etc.) which is really nothing but a Life of Adam, identical in great part with the Latin *Vita Adæ et Evæ*. Besides this there is a (late?) Hebrew *Apocalypse*, of Moses' progress through the seven heavens.

What of the *Testament* ? There is one`express quota-tion from it in a Greek catena on the Octateuch, giving the dimensions of the Tower of Babel, and this proves to be a quotation of *Jubilees*. Some therefore think the *Testament* to be *Jubilees* under yet another name : the obstacle is that 1100 lines is far too small a total for *Jubilees*. Dr. Charles differs. He thinks the *Testament* is that last dying speech of Moses, part of which we have in Latin and usually call the *Assumption*. In his view the *Assumption* proper was amalgamated at an early date with the *Testament*, and the two books circulated under the title of the *Assumption*. All the Latin frag-ment belongs to the *Testament*. Early the amalgamation must have been, for Jude quotes both parts in the first century (or at least early in the second). His 9th verse is, Origen tells us, from the *Assumption*, and his 16th we find in the Latin fragment.

The question is a difficult one. We will return to it, after collecting the fragments of the lost *Assumption* proper.

Let it be premised that in the spurious Acts of the Council of Nice by Gelasius Cyzicenus there is a dialogue between the Fathers and a Pagan philosopher. The Fathers twice quote the *Assumption* by name. First they give the text which stands in our Latin fragment as i. 14 : " God foresaw me before the foundation of the world to be the mediator of His covenant." Then, after a few pages, they say : " And in the Book of the *Assumption of Moses* Michael the Archangel, speaking with the devil, says, " For from His holy Spirit all we were created." And again he says : " From the face of God His Spirit went forth, and the world was." The philosopher says : " As to this *Assumption of Moses* which you quote, and of which you have just spoken, I never heard of it until now, so I beg you to expound to me more clearly the connexion of what is said." But no more light is given.

Jude 9, as is well known, is stated by Clement of Alexandria and Origen and Didymus to be a citation from the *Assumption*. " But Michael the archangel, when, contending with the devil, he disputed about the body of Moses, durst not bring against him a railing. accusation, but said, ' The Lord rebuke thee.' "

Origen (*De Principiis*, iii. 2) : " The serpent in Genesis is represented as deceiving Eve, *à propos* of which, in the *Ascension of Moses* (a book · mentioned by the Apostle Jude in his Epistle), Michael the archangel, disputing with the devil about the body of Moses, says that the serpent, inspired by the devil, was the cause of the transgression of Adam and Eve."

These are *certain* quotations. So are the next three, but the source is not named. Clement of Alexandria, *Strom.* vi., xv. (§ 132, p. 498, Stähelin) :

" With good reason, then, did Jesus the son of Naüe behold Moses being taken up in two forms, the one *companying* with angels, the other being honoured with burial in the glens of the mountains. But Jesus saw this sight below *him*, being lifted up by the spirit, with Chaleb also : but not in like manner do they both behold, but the one descended rather quickly, since he bore with him much that weighed him down, while the other, descending after him, related subsequently the glory which he beheld, having been able to discern more than the other, inasmuch as he was purer. The story indicates, I suppose, that *gnosis* is not for every man, since some look to the body of the Scriptures, the words and names, *corresponding to* the body of Moses, and others discern the thought, and what is signified by the names : such are concerned with the Moses who *companied* with angels.

" . . . The story about Moses teaches that contemplation is not given in full even to those in whom knowledge is at home, until, grown accustomed to looking directly at it, as the Hebrews on the glory of Moses and the holy men of Israel upon visions of angels, we become able to gaze upon the flashing light of truth."

Two other passages speak of the same episode : Origen (*on Joshua* ii. 1) : " In a certain book, though it be not in the canon, a figure of this mystery is described. It is related that two Moses' were seen, one alive in the spirit, the other dead in the body; wherein of course this is indicated, that if thou look at the bare letter of the law, empty of all the things that we have mentioned, that is Moses dead in the body : but if thou canst take away the veil of the law, and understand that the law is spiritual, that is Moses who liveth in the spirit."

Evodius, Bishop of Uzala, writing to Augustine (Ep. 258) : " In the apocryphal and the secret books of Moses himself—a writing without authority—when he went up into the mountain to die, such violence was done to his body (or the might of his body was such : *vi corporis efficitur ut*) that there was one *body* which was committed to the earth, and another which was joined with an angel as companion."

Next we come to a class of passages which relate to the contest of Michael with Satan.

Severus, Patriarch of Antioch (542), quoted in the *Catena* of Nicephorus on Deut. xxxiv., begins by saying that upon the parting of the soul from the body, good and evil angels meet it ; each band claiming it for their own in virtue of its deeds done in the body; and continues : " God, willing to show this also to the children of Israel by means of a bodily image, ordained that at the burial of Moses there should appear before their eyes at the time of the dressing (περιστολή) of the body and its due depositing in the earth, the evil demon as it were resisting and opposing; and that Michael, a good angel, should encounter and repel him, and should not rebuke him on his own authority, but retire from giving judgment against him in favour of the Lord of All, saying, ' The Lord rebuke thee,' in order that those who are being instructed in the word might learn that a measure of conflict awaits souls after their departure hence . . . further, when this heavenly image had come before their eyes, there came a cloud or light about the place which dazzled the eyes of the onlookers, and walled his grave off, that they might not see it. Therefore also it says in the Scripture, ' No man hath seen his end, or his grave, unto this day.' This, it is said, is set forth in an apocryphal book which contains the more detailed

account (λεπτοτέραν ἀφήγησιν) of the genesis or creation." These last words are an undoubted reference—
whether a correct one or not we shall have to consider—
to the *Leptogenesis* or *Book of Jubilees*.

Two other passages of Severus (who seems to have
been attracted by the subject) are given in *Catenæ* on
Jude.

" Michael is said to have ministered about the burial
of the body of Moses, when the devil withstood this, by
the permission of God, who wished by this manifesta-
tion to show them, who then were short of sight and dull
of understanding," that evil powers meet the soul after
death.

" Contending with the devil—a blasphemer and
fighter against God from the beginning : from the time
when he was infected with apostasy and after that
deceived Adam (and) by craft fought against the
commandment of God."

The anonymous extracts in *Catenæ* and marginal
scholia of MSS. are many : I will give one here from a
good Greek MS. (Bodl. Arch. E 5, 9) which sums up almost
all the matter of the others.

It is a *scholium* on Jude 9.

" Hereby he shows that the Old Testament agrees
with the New, both being given by one God. For the
devil resisted, trying to deceive, saying, ' The body is
mine, for I am the Lord of matter,' and was answered
by ' The Lord rebuke thee '—that is, the Lord who is
Master of all spirits. Others say that God, willing to
show that after our departure hence demons oppose
our souls on their upward course, permitted this to be
beheld at the burial of Moses. For the devil also blas-
phemed against Moses, calling him a murderer because
he smote the Egyptian. Michael the Archangel, not
enduring his blasphemy, said to him, ' The Lord God
rebuke thee, devil.' He also said this, that God had
lied by bringing Moses into the land which He swore
he should not enter."

The other notes add nothing to this, except it be one
sentence with which some begin, viz.: " When Moses

had died in the mount, Michael was sent to remove the body." Several of them read " God rebuke thee," instead of " the Lord," and this *might* be a quotation from the *Assumption*.

Next I place two accounts of the death of Moses. The first is from the Greek *Palæa*, a popular Bible-history of Byzantine times, which is the Eastern equivalent of the *Historia Scholastica* (of Petrus Comestor, cent. xii.), which, with the French version, the *Bible Historiale*, was so common in the West. The text of the *Palæa*, printed by Vassiliev in *Anecdota Græco-Byzantina*, has this passage (p. 247) :

" *Of the death of Moses.* And Moses said unto Jesus the son of Naüë, ' Let us go up into the mountain.' And when they were gone up, Moses saw the land of promise and said to Jesus, ' Go down unto the people and tell them " Moses is dead." ' And Jesus went down unto the people, but Moses came to the end of his life. And Samael tried to bring down his body (tabernacle) unto the people, that they might make him a god. But Michael, the Chief Captain, by the command of God came to take him and bury him, and Samael resisted him, and they contended. So the Chief Captain was wroth and rebuked him, saying, ' The Lord rebuke thee, devil.' And so the adversary was vanquished and took to flight, but the Archangel Michael buried the body of Moses where he was bidden by Christ our God (and no man saw the burial of Moses)."

The second is from the Slavonic *Life of Moses* translated by Bonwetsch in the Göttingen *Nachrichten* for 1900, pp. 581–607. This *Life* for the most part follows Jewish tradition very closely, and has the familiar additions to the story which we find in Josephus.

After mentioning the deaths of Miriam and Aaron, it says :

" But at the end of the same year in the 2nd (*sic*) month Nadet, on the 7th day (that is in March), Moses the servant of God died and was buried on the 4th of the month September on a certain mountain by the Chief Captain Michael. For the devil contended with

the angel, and would not permit his body to be buried,
saying, ' Moses is a murderer. He slew a man in Egypt
and hid him in the sand.' Then Michael prayed to
God and there was thunder and lightning and suddenly
the devil disappeared; but Michael buried him with
his *own* hands.''

The mention of the thunder and lightning does occur
also in a Greek note which I have read in a recent German
comment on Jude, but unfortunately cannot now trace.

Two more passages exhaust my material.

Clement of Alexandria, *Strom.* i. 23 (§ 153, p. 95,
Stähelin) : " Moses was called Joacim. He had also
a third name in heaven after his assumption, as the
initiated (μύσται) say, viz. Melchi." Within a few lines
(§ 154, p. 96) he seems to quote the same authority
again. " The initiated (μύσται) say that he slew the
Egyptian merely with a word, as Peter slew Ananias
and Sapphira." We know that the slaying of the
Egyptian was part of the devil's claim against Moses in
the *Assumption*.

Epiphanius, *Hær.* 1 : " The angels, as the tradition
that has reached us tells, buried the body of the holy
Moses, and did not purify (wash) themselves, but the
angels were not made unclean (common) by the holy
body."

From these data a conjectural narrative may be put
together.

Moses dies in the Mount. Michael and other angels
are sent to bury him. They find Satan about to carry
off the body, and meaning to induce the people to worship
it. They contend with him, and he resists and says,
" The body is mine, for all material things belong to
me." " No," replies Michael. " By His Holy Spirit
all we were created," and, " From the face of God His
Spirit went forth and the world came into being."
Possibly at this time, too, Michael reproached him for
having brought sin into the world by inspiring the
serpent to deceive Adam and Eve. Then Satan said,
" Moses is a murderer, and must not be buried with
honour : he slew the Egyptian '' ; and again, " God has

lied in bringing Moses into the land which He swore he
should not enter." Michael, aghast at the blasphemy,
said, " The Lord rebuke thee." The Lord, in answer,
thundered and lightened out of heaven, and Satan fled.
There were some mortal spectators of the scene :
perhaps only Joshua and Caleb, perhaps the contest was
visible .to the people, as Severus seems to indicate, and
after that a cloud of light shut off their view. At any
rate, of what followed, Joshua and Caleb were the only
spectators, and one of them (almost certainly Joshua)
saw more than the other. Both were caught up into
the air, and below them they saw a wonderful spectacle :
there were two figures of Moses, one being laid in the
earth by angels in a mountain valley, the other, accom-
panied by angels, passing upwards to the heavens.
Caleb, who seems to have been ceremonially impure,
sank to the earth before Joshua : Joshua descended
after him and related what he had seen to the people.
He was able to tell them that the angels who had buried
Moses had contracted no ceremonial pollution by
touching that dead body, and also that he had heard a
new name of Moses proclaimed in heaven, namely,
Melchi.

Some points in the story are so interesting and unusual
that we must greatly regret the loss of the full text.

There is no doubt that the complexion of the Latin
fragment which we have is quite unlike what we have
of the *Assumption.* The one is wholly prophecy, and
dialogue with Joshua, the other is mystical romance.
So far Dr. Charles has a plausible case for his suggestion
that two books, originally separate, have been amalgamated. We have a parallel in the *Ascension of Isaiah,*
which consists of two distinct parts, the Martyrdom
and the Vision. The fashion has been to regard these
as originally distinct ; or rather, perhaps, to say that the
Vision is a later appendix to the Martyrdom. However, in this case Professor Burkitt (*Christian and Jewish
Apocalypses :* Schweich Lectures) has brought forward
strong grounds for believing that the book may really
be a unity : and I am on the whole prepared to follow

him in thinking (as he does) that the *Assumption of Moses* also originally contained both elements, of prophecy and romance. The amalgamation of the two, if it took place, must have been effected within a very short space. The prophecy is dated by Dr. Charles in the first century, and the Assumption story was joined with it, as we have seen, before Jude wrote his Epistle.

Dr. Charles asks, reasonably enough: If the title *Assumption* includes the Latin fragment, what was the *Testament?* Not the *Jubilees;* for that is far more than 1100 lines long—probably 4000 or 5000.

Well, we cannot go much behind our evidence. The *Catena* of Nicephorus quotes a piece which occurs in *Jubilees* and calls its source the *Testament.* We are reduced, I think, to supposing either that the number of lines in the MSS. of the Stichometry is grossly wrong, or that some excerpt or shortened text of *Jubilees* was current under the name of the *Testament of Moses.*

It seems clear that the *Jubilees* and the *Assumption* were circulated together. There are two pieces of evidence of this. The Milan palimpsest contains the Latin version of both : the versions of the two works were made, it appears, by different translators; but there they are together. Also Severus of Antioch, as we have seen, says that his source was the *Leptogenesis* (= *Jubilees*), but the story he has told relating to the death and burial of Moses and to the contention of Michael with Satan finds no place in *Jubilees*, whereas it was treated of in the *Assumption.* My inference is that he or his authority (for his expressions suggest that he is writing at second hand) used a volume in which both *Jubilees* and the *Assumption* were contained.

The Latin fragment, it is calculated, contains 384 whole *stichoi :* the *Assumption* (entire) had 1400. We appear to possess the whole, or very nearly the whole, of the Prophecy of Moses : the writer has brought his sketch of events down to and beyond his own time. The story of the *Assumption* might well occupy the 1000 *stichoi* that remain. But Dr. Charles supposes that the Latin fragment is the *Testament* (of 1100 *stichoi*), and that the *Assumption* of the lists is the second part, which was amalgamated with the *Testament*. I find it difficult to imagine how the 1100 *stichoi* of the *Testament* could have been filled up; and I think the lists are too late in date to be credited with preserving the tradition of the two books as separate. They were already joined in Jude's time; the lists, at a generous estimate, could hardly be older than the fourth century, and we are not sure that they are older than the sixth.

There is some reason for thinking that other Moses Apocrypha of a prophetic kind were current. The same passage of Gelasius Cyzicenus which gave us two sentences of the *Assumption* says (immediately after quoting the sentence about the mediator): "And in the Book of the Mystical Words of Moses, Moses himself predicted concerning David and Solomon, and of Solomon he predicted thus : ' And God shall give by inheritance unto him (διαδοχεύσει εἰσ αὐτόν) wisdom and justice and full knowledge : he shall build the house of God,' and what follows." It is just possible that the writer here may be ignorantly quoting one book under two names, or employing two sources; compare the " mystic words " of the title with Clement's use of (μύσται) " initiated," where he is to all appearance quoting the *Assumption*. In any case, we never hear of *The Book of Mystic Words* again.

One of the most considerable Greek magical texts that the papyri have given us purports to be a secret Book of Moses, the Eighth. It is printed by Dieterich in *Abraxas*. A Hebrew magical text, the *Sword of Moses*, has been edited by Dr. M. Gaster, as well as an *Apocalypse*, a vision of the next world. A *Colloquy of the Prophet Moses with God*, of Christian complexion, was printed by Lord Zouche of Parham (Hon. R. Curzon) from a MS. in his possession, and again by Isaac Hall in the American periodical *Hebraica*, 1891.

SOLOMON

The principal Apocrypha current under this name are the famous *Book of Wisdom*, the *Psalms and Odes*, the

E

less known *Testament*, a number of quite late magical books, and a dialogue with the Queen of Sheba (tr. Issaverdens).

There is a romance, too, in Slavonic, the story of Solomon and Kitovras, of which I know no version in a readable language, and this is connected with the dialogue-literature that goes under Solomon's name in the *Salomon and Saturn* and *Salomon and Marcolphus*. The latter exists in most European vernaculars, and, as time goes on, becomes more and more coarse and burlesque. The former, *Salomon and Saturn*, is best represented by certain Anglo-Saxon texts which Kemble edited with a valuable collection of illustrative documents for the Ælfric Society, while A. von Vincenti issued the prolegomena of a new edition in 1904. I cannot tell whether his work has been completed.

This *Salomon and Saturn* is mentioned here because I believe it to be the text called in the *Gelasian Decree* the *Interdictio* or *Contradictio Salomonis*. It is not universally allowed to be the same. Kemble thought it was. The *Interdictio* is mentioned in the decree along with magical "phylacteries," and some have thought that it was a magical text.

The case cannot be positively settled by any evidence we have at present. Whether or not, however, the *Salomon and Saturn* is identical with the *Interdictio*, it represents an old book, and a strange one.

The first portion, partly in verse and partly in prose, is occupied with a description of the glories of the "Palm-twigged Paternoster" (the prayer being personified) and of the combat between the devil and the Paternoster. This is quite unique, so far as I know. Then we have a second part in verse, which is in the riddle form, predominantly. In it is that possible allusion to the story of Og which has been quoted, and also a curious description of a monstrous bird called *Vasa Mortis ;* most of the questions, however, relate to life and morals. It is fairly certain, says Vincenti (p. 124), that a Latin original lies behind the poem. If he is right, the case would be like that of the amazing

Irish book called the *Evernew Tongue,* where a Latin original has been overlaid, thickly, by Celtic imagery. (See *J. T. S.,* 1918.)

Very different in character is the prose Anglo-Saxon *Salomon and Saturn,* which asks such questions as, which is the blessedest bird, where the sun sets, who first planted the vine, etc., etc. Of this pedestrian class of catechisms there are many specimens in East and West, running down to the very end of the mediæval period, and beyond it. The whole class deserves collection and examination, from the pagan and philosophical dialogue of Hadrian and Secundus to the " Master of Oxenford's" Catechism.

ELIJAH. APOCALYPSE

Elias. The list of the Sixty Books speaks of the *Apocalypse of Elias.* The other two have simply " Of Elias the Prophet." The Latin version of the stichometry, by Anastasius Bibliothecarius, renders " Prophecy of Elias." The Armenian has " The Mysteries of Elias." The stichometry gives it 316 lines.

To this book, two passages in St. Paul's Epistles are referred. The first is 1 Cor. ii. 9: " Eye hath not seen," etc. Origen (*on Matt.* xxvii. 9) says : " This is found in no canonical book, but in the apocrypha (*in secretis*) of Elias." Jerome (Ep. 101 to Pammachius), with his eye on Origen, no doubt, writes : " In this place some will follow after the drivellings of apocryphal writings and say that the quotation is taken from the *Apocalypse of Elias,* whereas we read thus in Isaiah according to the Hebrew, ' From everlasting they have not heard,' etc. (Isa. lxiv. 4)." And again, in his great commentary on Isaiah (lib. xvii.) he fulminates against this view, contorting Ps. x. 3, and making it say " the devil lies in wait in the Apocrypha," after which he adds, " for the *Ascension of Isaiah* and the *Apocalypse of Elias* have this quotation."

The truth about the quotation seems to be (as Mr. H. St. J. Thackeray has shown in *St. Paul and Contemporary Jewish Thought,* p. 240) that it was a blend of passages from Isaiah (lxiv. 4, lxv. 16, 17) in current use in the first century. Pseudo-Philo has it (xxvi. 13), and this makes it easier to believe that Origen was right when he said it occurred in the *Apocalypse of Elias*. It is also found, as Jerome says, in the *Ascension of Isaiah* (xi. 34), but in the Latin and Slavonic, not the Ethiopic version.

Resch, in his *Agrapha*, p. 154 *ff.*, has a long disquisition on the subject, and among the parallels he adduces is one which deserves to be repeated here. Clement of Alexandria (*Protrept.*, § 44, p. 69, Stähelin, 76, Potter) has this passage : " Wherefore the Scripture with reason makes this promise to them that have believed : ' but the Saints of the Lord shall inherit the glory of God and His power.' " " Tell me what glory, O blessed one ? " " That which eye hath not seen, nor ear heard, neither hath it come up upon the heart of man : and they shall rejoice at the kingdom (ἐπὶ τῇ βασιλείᾳ) of their Lord for ever. Amen." This is apparently the conclusion of a book : with it we should compare (as Resch does) a passage in the *Apostolical Constitutions* (vii. 32, p. 212), which is an amplification of the end of the *Didache*, and runs thus :

" Then shall the wicked depart into everlasting punishment : but the righteous shall go into life eternal, inheriting those things which eye hath not seen, nor ear heard, neither have they come up upon the heart of man, which God hath prepared for them that love Him, and shall rejoice in the Kingdom of God in Christ Jesus."

The other Pauline passage referred to this book is Ephesians v. 14 : " Awake, thou that sleepest," etc., of which Epiphanius (*Hær.* xlii. 1) says : " This is contained in Elias." Others derive it from a book of Jeremiah, as we shall see. Hippolytus (*on Daniel* iv. 56) gives it to Isaiah, where Esaias *may* be an error for Elias. There is nothing to confirm or invalidate Epiphanius's statement.

Two other fragments definitely attributed to the *Apocalypse of Elias* have made their appearance in recent years.

One is in a very curious Latin document, itself apocryphal, which is entitled *The Epistle of Titus, the disciple of Paul*, and is preserved in an eighth-century MS. at Würzburg. It has not been printed as a whole, but Dom. D. de Bruyn, O.S.B., has published in the *Revue Bénédictine* (1900, pp. 149–160) a number of apocryphal quotations from it. One is this: " The prophet Helias bears witness that he saw : ' The angel of the Lord,' saith he, ' showed me a deep valley which is called Gehenna, burning with sulphur and pitch, and in that place are many souls of sinners, and thus are they tortured with divers torments. Some suffer hanging . . . by their tongues, some by their eyes, others hang head downward; women will be tormented by their breasts, and youths hanging by their hands; certain maidens are burned upon a gridiron and some souls are fixed (? pierced) with perpetual pain. Now by these divers torments is shown the act of every one. . . . They that hang by the tongues are blasphemers and also false witnesses : they that are burned (*read* hung by) their eyes are they that have [been] offended in regard of sight, because they looked upon things done guiltily in concupiscence : but they that hang head downwards, these are they that hated the righteousness of God, being of evil counsel, neither did any agree with his brother : rightly, therefore, are they burned (? hung) by the decree of punishment (*lit.* punishment of decree). But whereas women are commanded to be tormented in their breasts, these are they which gave their bodies unto men in lasciviousness, wherefore the men also will be hard by them in torments, hanging by their hands upon this account."

My version tries to give an idea of the obscurity and badness of the Latin. The passage shows that part of the Apocalypse at least dealt with visions of the next world, and that in it hell-torments were described (as they are in the *Apocalypse of Peter*), as suited to the sin of the sufferer. This fashion rules in a whole series of later Christian Apocalypses; but it is a deduction from the *lex talionis* and is exemplified in writings undoubtedly Jewish. Thus in the *Chronicles of Jerah-meel* (tr. M. Gaster, 1899, pp. 34–36) are two revelations which agree most closely with our fragment.

(*a*) R. Joshua, son of Levi, said, " I was walking on my way when I met the prophet Elijah. He said to me, ' Would you like to be brought to the gate of hell? ' I answered, ' Yes.' So he showed me men hanging by their hair, and he said to me, ' These were the men that let their hair grow to adorn themselves for sin ' (*men* is very likely a mistake here for *women*). The other classes of sinners were these :

Others hanging by their eyes.	Followed their eyes to sin.
By their noses.	Perfumed themselves to sin.
By their tongues.	Had slandered.
By their hands.	Had stolen.
Ignominiously.	
By their feet.	Led men to sin.
Women hanging by their breasts.	Had exposed them to make men sin.
Men fried on fiery coals.	Had blasphemed.
Men fed on gall, etc.	Had eaten on fast days.

(*b*) " There are five kinds of punishments in hell, and Isaiah the son of Amoz saw them all. He entered the first compartment and saw there two men carrying pails full of water on their shoulders, and they that water into a pit which never fills. Isaiah said to God, ' O thou who unveilest all that is hidden, unveil to me the secret of this.' And the spirit of the Lord answered, ' These are the men who coveted the property of their neighbours, and this is their punishment.' The formula is the same in the next three sections.

Men hanging by their tongues.	Slanderers.
Hanging ignominiously.	
Women hanging by their breasts.	Attracted the gaze of men.

" The fifth section is not of the same form. The compartment is full of smoke and the princes, chiefs and great men are in it, presided over by Pharaoh."

It will be noticed that the former of these visions

is actually connected with Elijah and is closer to the Latin fragment than the second.

My other fragment was printed in the *Journal Asiatique*, 1917, p. 454, by Abbé F. Nau from a Paris MS. (gr. 4) of the thirteenth century. It occurs along with an extract from the *Revelation of (pseudo) Methodius*, and some descriptions of Antichrist from Chrysostom and from the Bible and elsewhere.

" It is contained in apocryphal writings that Elias the prophet spake concerning Antichrist, of what aspect he is to appear at that time. His head a flame of fire : his right eye mingled with blood, but the left bright (χάροπόσ) having two pupils : his eyebrows (-lashes) white, and his lower lip large : his right thigh thin and his feet broad, and the great toe of his foot hath been broken."

Something, nearly identical with this description of Antichrist is to be found in several other places, in the *Testament of the Lord* (Syriac) xi., in the *Testament in Galilee* (ed. Guerrier and Grébaut, Ethiopic), 6, and in a Latin fragment from Trèves printed by me in *Apocrypha anecdota* (i., p. 153). I show them in tabular form.

Test. of the Lord	*Test. in Galilee*	*Latin Fragment*
His head as a burn-ing flame.	Head as a flame of fire.	His eyes " *fellini* " like a cat's (?).
Right eye mingled with blood.	Right eye mingled with blood.	Right eye mingled with blood.
Left eye of a blue-grey or green colour having two pupils.	Left eye dead. The two pupils of the eyes are \<*gup*\>	Left eye joyful (*gaudens* — χαροπόσ).
Eyelashes white.	White in his eye-lids.	Eyelashes white.
Lower lip large.	Lower lip large.	Lower lip large.
Right thigh thin.	*Omitted.*	† His legs lean.
Feet broad.	"	*Omitted.*
Great toe broken and oblong (or thin).	Toes and joints of his feet twisted.	Great toe broken.
He is the scythe of desolation.	He is the scythe of perdition.	He is the scythe of desolation.

The portion of the two *Testaments* which contains this description is generally taken to be a separate Apocalypse. In each case it is followed by matter of a quite different kind, in the *Testament of the Lord* by rules of ecclesiastical practice, in the *Testament in Galilee* by an Epistle of the Apostles. It does occur separately in Syriac in a Cambridge MS. edited by Arendzen (in *Jour. Theol. Stud.*, ii., 1901, p. 401). The only notable variant in the description of Antichrist which this presents is at the end ("his feet broad and his little finger large as a sickle—that is, the sickle of desolation"), and this is probably a mistake.

Cap. XI. of this Apocalypse deals with the misfortunes of individual countries—Syria, Cilicia, and so on (this is omitted in Arendzen's text), and as Arendzen remarks in his preface (see also Bidez in his edition of Philostorgius), the description comes very close to that given by Philostorgius in his *Church History* of the actual events of the early part of the fifth century. The Apocalypse is not, in any case, as a whole, very early in date, and there is no reason to doubt that it incorporated older material, and that some of this came from the *Apocalypse of Elias*.

The description of Antichrist which we have here is but one of many. The late Greek Apocalypses of Esdras and of John edited by Tischendorf contain another, or rather two others (one in MSS. of both *Esdras* and *John*, the other in a Venice MS. of *John*), which may as well be given:

Esdras-John	*John* (Venice MS.)
The likeness of his face is dark.	
The hairs of his head sharp as arrows.	The hairs of his head like sharpened arrows.
His eyebrows like a field.	His teeth a span long.
His right eye like the morning star.	His legs like a cock's.
The other immovable (*or* like a lion's).	The sole of his feet two spans long.
His mouth about a cubit long.	His eyebrows full of all foulness and roughness.
His teeth a span long.	
His fingers like sickles.	On his forehead a writing: Antichrist.

Esdras-John	*John* (Venice MS.)
The sole of his feet two spans long.	Holding in his right hand a cup of death.
On his forehead a writing: Antichrist.	One eye like the morning star, the other like a lion's (it
Sometimes he will become a child.	was "quenched" when he fell, by Christ).
And sometimes an old man.	

The Armenian *Seventh Vision of Daniel* (tr. Issaverdens, p. 345) says:
"The joints of his knees are stiff, he is crippled in body, smooth-browed, crooked-fingered, long-headed, charming, boastful, intelligent, etc., etc."

A Latin text, a prophecy of our Lord addressed to St. Matthew, which I have only found in one MS. (*Corpus Chr. Coll. Camb.*, 404, f. 7 (fourteenth century); see my *Catalogue*, ii. 270), says: "His appearance (*positio*) will be, a thin and tall man, with thin feet, having long hair and a long face and a long nose, with cat's eyes: † in the lower parts † having lost one tooth, in the upper marked with leprosy, having a white part in the hair on his forehead. These his marks will be unchangeable, but in the others he will be able to change himself." This shows interesting coincidences with the Latin fragment and with the Coptic and Hebrew Elias (below). It is corrupt, some words having apparently dropped out.

Similar descriptions also occur in late Hebrew Apocalypses such as the *Book of Zerubbabel* (see Bossuet, *Antichrist*, p. 102): the *Midrash Vajoscha* says, "He will be bald, and have one eye large and one small, his right arm will be a span long and his left two and a half ells: on his forehead will be leprosy, his right ear will be stopped up and his left open."

But to come nearer to the point again. We have two *Apocalypses of Elias*, and in each of them is a description of Antichrist: only neither agrees with that which we have read in the Greek fragment.

The first, which is almost complete, is in Coptic, existing in imperfect MSS. in two dialects, Achmimic and Sahidic, edited by Steindorff (1899). A very small bit of it (corresponding to ll. 6–13 of p. 169) has been found in a Greek papyrus (*Papiri greci e latini*, Florence, 1912, No. 7). It consists of two parts: the beginning is moral and didactic, and speaks of fasting and so on; then there is an abrupt change, and the text continues: "Concerning the King of the Assyrians and the dissolution of the Heaven and Earth: My people shall not

be overpowered, saith the Lord, and shall not need to
be afraid in war." And the rest is wholly eschatological : rise and fall of kings, appearances of Antichrist :
his conflict with Tabitha, death of Elias (!) and Enoch,
the end of the world, are treated in detail. The
introduction of Elias is, to say the least, inartistic.

The description of Antichrist is this : " He is little . . .
young, thin-legged, on his forehead is a place of white
hair . . . his eyebrows stretch to his ears, he has
marks of leprosy in his hands. He will change himself
before them that look on him, will become a child and
an old man . . . will change in all his marks; but
the marks on his head . . . will not be able to be
changed." There are more coincidences here with the
Esdras-John descriptions than with the Greek fragment.

The other *Apocalypse of Elias* is a late Hebrew one
edited by Buttenwieser (1897), who believes that events
of about A.D. 260 are described in it : I should be
surprised if it were really so ancient, in its present
rather incoherent form, but it probably has some
connexion with the older Apocalypse. Especially, I
think, does this apply to the opening, the substance of
which is this :

" The Spirit took me up and bore me to the South :
I saw a high place burning with fire, which none could
enter.

" It bore me to the East : there I saw stars fighting
with each other unceasingly.

" It bore me to the West : there I saw how souls
suffered judgment in great torments, *each one according
to his deeds.*

" Then Michael revealed to me the End."

Then we plunge into prophecy, with names of kings
and cities, days of the month, and large hosts, whose
numbers are given. Near the beginning is the description of Antichrist. " These will be his signs, as Daniel
beheld him : his face is long, on his forehead he has
baldness (?), and he is of very high stature, and his
feet are high, and his legs are thin."

The first sentence reads like a summary of a longer

writing, and the words I have italicized show where something like our Latin fragment might have come in. It is quite probable, I think, that the original Apocalypse contained all the ingredients that the fragments show us, descriptions of hell-torments, eschatological prophecy, descriptions of Antichrist and didactic matter. But neither of the extant Apocalypses can be supposed to represent the old book faithfully. The Coptic has been Christianized, the Hebrew abridged, and additions made to both.

In the *Lives of the Prophets*, attributed to Epiphanius, there is a bit of legend about Elijah which reads as if it might have originally stood in an apocryphal book. That apocryphal literature was to some extent employed by the writer of these Lives is considered probable or even certain by their latest editor, Schermann, on the evidence of the sections relating to Isaiah and Jeremiah, though, for much of the non-Biblical detail, current Jewish tradition may be responsible.

The life of Elias begins : " He was of Thesbis, of the land of the Arabs, of the tribe of Aaron, dwelling in Galaad; for Thesbis was a gift, given to the priests. And when his mother bore him, Sobac his father saw a vision, that men shining in white spoke to him (the child), and that they swaddled him in fire and gave him a flame of fire to eat. And he went to Jerusalem and told the priests, and the oracle said : Fear not, for the habitation of this child shall be light, and his word a decree, and he shall judge Israel in the sword and in fire."

Another legend, common to Chrysostom (*in Petrum et Eliam*) and the Armenian Life of Elias (tr. Issaverdens), may well be only an embellishment of the Bible narrative. It is that at the sacrifice on Carmel the priests of Baal secreted a man under their altar with orders to light the fire at the proper moment, but that he was either suffocated or died at the word of Elias, who divined his presence.

Jeremiah

All the four major prophets have had spurious books fathered upon them. For *Isaiah* we have the extant *Ascension of Isaiah;* for Jeremiah the *Paralipomena of Jeremiah*, current in Greek, Ethiopic, and Armenian, and edited by Dr. Rendel Harris under its alternative title, *The Rest of the Words of Baruch.* We have also some scattered quotations attributed to him. In Matt. xxvii. 9 the prophecy, "And they took the thirty pieces of silver," etc., is, as we all know, assigned to Jeremiah. Origen (*in loc.*) suspects either a mistake (Jeremiah for Zechariah) or the existence of some apocryphal writing of Jeremiah in which the words occurred. Jerome (*in loc.*) had actually seen such a thing. "I lately read in a Hebrew book, which a Hebrew of the Nazarene sect showed me, an apocryph of Jeremiah in which I found this, word for word." We know of no continuous text comprising these words, but there is current in Ethiopic, usually appended to the canonical Book of Jeremiah, a short prophecy, which Dillmann prints and translates in his *Chrestomathia Æthiopica*, p. viii. I believe it to exist also in Coptic.

"A Prophecy of Jeremiah. And Jeremiah spake thus unto Pashur : But ye all your days fight against the truth, with your fathers and your sons that shall come after you. And they shall commit a sin more damnable than you : they shall sell him who hath no price, and shall hurt him who will heal pain, and shall condemn him who will forgive sin, and shall take thirty pieces of silver, the price of him that was valued, whom the children of Israel shall sell, and shall give that money for (into) the potter's field. As the Lord commanded me, so I speak. And therefore shall there come upon them judgment and destruction for ever, and upon their sons after them, because in their judgment they have shed innocent blood."

Nothing can be more obvious than that this was written to set right the difficulty caused by the mention

of Jeremiah in the Gospel.   It may quite well be identical with the writing seen by Jerome.   His interest in
such things was not lively enough to make him use
accurate language :   he is oftener contemptuous and
angry when apocryphal writings come into his ken.
    Eph. v. 14, " Awake, thou that sleepest," etc., is said
by George the Syncellus to be quoted " from what are
called the Apocrypha of Jeremiah," and this attribution is found in a marginal note in some MSS. of the
Epistles :   one authority names the *Paralipomena of
Jeremiah*, but, though an important part of that story
is the seventy years' sleep of Ebed-melech and his
awaking at the Return of the People from Babylon,
the words of *Ephesians* are not in our texts of this book.
Hippolytus (*on Antichrist*, 65) quotes them as said by
" the prophet," and (*on Daniel* iv. 56) as from Isaiah.
We have seen that Epiphanius assigns them to Elias.
    Then there is a passage which Justin Martyr (*Dial.
with Trypho*) accuses the Jews of having deleted from
the Book of Jeremiah.   He says it was still to be found
in some synagogue copies, so that its deletion must
have been recent.   Irenæus also quotes it not less than
four times in varying forms, once as from Isaiah, once
as from Jeremiah, and twice without naming the
prophet.   Justin's form, the only one we have in
Greek, is :
    " And the Lord God of Israel remembered the dead
which slept in the dust of the earth, and came down
unto them to preach (evangelize) His salvation."
    In the Latin *Acts of St. James the Great*, which form
Book IV of the so-called *Historia Apostolica* of Abdias,
in a speech of St. James to the Jews, several Messianic
prophecies are quoted, and among them this :
    " Jeremiah   adds :   Behold,   O   Jerusalem,   thy
redeemer cometh, and this shall be his sign.   He shall
open the eyes of the blind and restore hearing to the
deaf, and by his voice he shall raise the dead."
    In a similar anti-Jewish oration of St. Silvester in
his *Acts* (I quote from the text of George Cedrenus) is
this :

"And that He shall be buried also, Jeremias saith :
By (in) his burying the dead shall be made alive."
Of these three obviously Christian passages it is
difficult to say whether all are taken from an apocryphal
book or were Christian interpolations into the text of
the LXX. To the Justin passage this last explanation
probably does apply. As to the Silvester passage, I
note that it immediately follows one from Esdras
which is to be found in the best text of 4 *Esdras* i.
This is a presumption (slight enough) in favour of the
view that it was at least not invented by the writer of
the Acts. As to the quotation in St. James's Acts, I
am left quite doubtful : but here again it is the only
prophecy cited which cannot be found in the Bible.

EZEKIEL

More is to be said about Ezekiel. I have elsewhere
(*J. T. S.* xv. 236, 1914) put together what I could
find on the subject of the apocryphal Book of Ezekiel.
The passages shall be translated here.

The most important is a parable which is quoted by
Epiphanius (*Hær.* lxiv. 10), who is writing against
the Origenists and discussing the resurrection of the
body. " For the dead shall rise and they that are in
the sepulchre shall be raised," says the prophet (cf.
Isa. xxvi. 19). And, for I must not pass over in
silence what is said by Ezekiel the prophet in his own
apocryphal book (*i. e.* that under his name) about
resurrection, I will quote the very passage here. For,
telling a·story in cryptic (enigmatic) guise, he says
about the just judgment in which soul and body *both*
share, that a certain King had all the men in his kingdom
enrolled in the army and had no " pagan " (" civilian,"
we should say), but two only, one lame and one blind,
and each abode separately and dwelt apart. And the
King made a marriage-feast for his own son and invited
all that were in his kingdom, but neglected the two
pagani, the lame man and the blind. And they were
angry in themselves and set about contriving a design

against the King. Now the King had a garden : and the blind man called out from a distance to the lame man and said, " How much would the breaking of our bread have been (What would have been the extra cost of entertaining us) with the multitudes that are invited to the merry-making? Come then, and as he hath done to us, let us requite him." The other asked, " In what way?" and he said, " Let us go into his garden and destroy the things there." But he said, " And how can I, who am lame and cannot walk? " and the blind man said, " What can I myself do, who cannot see whither I am going? but let us devise means." (Then the lame man) plucked the grass that was near him and plaited a rope and threw it to the blind man and said, " Catch hold of it and come along the rope hither to me." And when he had done as he was told and was come to the place, the lame man said, " Come, be feet to me and carry me, and I will be eyes to thee from above and guide thee to the right hand and the left." And so they did, and went down to the garden. Then, for the rest, whether they spoiled it or not, at all events their tracks were to be seen in the garden. And when the feasters dispersed from the marriage, they went into the garden and were enraged at finding the tracks there, and reported it to the King, saying, " We are all soldiers in thy kingdom, and there is no *paganus*. Whence, then, are the track of *pagani* in the garden? " And he marvelled. And as the parable—that of the apocryphal book, I mean—puts it, it applies to a man, but God is not ignorant of anything. But the story says that the King sent for the lame and the blind man, and asked the blind man, " Didst thou go down into the garden? " And he said, " Alas, Lord ! thou seest our infirmity : thou knowest that I cannot see where I walk." Then he came to the lame man and asked him, " Didst thou go down into my garden?" and he answered and said, " O Lord, wouldest thou afflict my soul in respect of my infirmity? " And then the judgment was at a standstill. What, then, does the just judge do? Having discerned in what manner the two were yoked together, he sets the lame man on the blind man's back, and examines both of them with scourges, and they cannot deny the fact. Each convicts the other, the lame man saying to the blind, " Didst thou not bear me and carry me off?" and the blind to the lame, " Didst not thou thyself become eyes to me?" In like manner, the body is joined with the soul and the soul with the body to convict them of their deeds done in common, and the judgment becomes complete from (for) both of them, body and soul, of the works they have done, whether good or bad.

A little later on Epiphanius returns to the parable and probably embodies in what he says the gist of the interpretation of it.

He says: God cannot separate the soul from the body for the purpose of final judgment. " For immediately the judgment will be found at a standstill. For if the soul be found all by itself, it would reply when judged, ' The cause of sin is not of me, but of that corruptible and earthly body, in fornication, adultery, lasciviousness. For since it left me, I have done none of these things,' and it will have a good defence and will paralyze the judgment of God.'. . . The body cannot be judged apart from the soul : for it also could reply, saying, ' It was not I that sinned, it was the soul : have I, since it departed from me, committed adultery, fornicated, or worshipped idols?' and the body will be withstanding the justice of God, and with reason. On this account, therefore . . . God . . . brings our dead bodies and our souls to a second birth," etc.

This parable is found current in Rabbinic tradition. Three versions of it are given in a book by Fiebig (*Die Gleichnisreden Jesu im Lichte der Rabbinischen Gleichnisse der N.T. lichen Zeitalters*, p. 73). One is ascribed to R. Ishmael (*cir.* A.D. 130), the other two to R. Jehuda (*cir.* 200). Here the lame and blind are custodians of the King's garden and their transgression is eating the choice early fruits. There is nothing about the wedding-feast or the soldiers and *pagani.*

The application is the same. The soul will say, "I
have not sinned; it is the body. Since I came out from
it I have been like a pure bird that flies in the air."
The body says, "I have not sinned; it is the soul.
Since it went forth from me I have been like a stone
that is thrown on the ground."
Whether this is a later or an earlier form of the
story than Ezekiel's, it seems to me an inferior one.
The next fragment is very short. Tertullian (de
Carne Christi, 23) says : "We read indeed in Ezekiel
about that cow which bare and bare not : but consider
whether the Holy Spirit did not even then blame you
by that utterance, foreseeing that you would dispute
over the womb of Mary."
We have the quotation elsewhere, but only here is
the source of it named. Thus Epiphanius (Hær.
xxx. 20) : "Behold, the virgin shall be with child
and bear a son." He said not,." Behold, the woman " :
and again in another place he saith, "And the heifer
shall bear, and they shall say, ' She hath not borne ' ;
for because some of the Manichæans and Marcionites
say, ' He was not born,' therefore is it said, ' She shall
bear,' and they shall say, ' She hath not borne.' "
The old Acts of Peter, 29, quote several prophecies
(including one from the Ascension of Isaiah) : "And
again he saith, ' She hath borne and hath not borne,' "
is one of these.
Clement of Alexandria (Str. vii. 16, p. 66, Stähelin)
has the same words, with " saith the Scripture."
Gregory of Nyssa (Adversus Judæos, 3), " And again :
Behold, the heifer hath borne and hath not borne."
Tertullian's words seem to imply that there was
some story attached to the saying. It might very well
have been a parable. In fact, as it stands it is a
parable. I do not see that it can have been anything
but Christian; the application to the Virgin-Birth
must have been intended by the writer.
A third phrase which is quoted again and again by
Fathers of all ages, and sometimes as a saying of
Christ's, is attributed in the Life of St. Antony to Ezekiel,

F

and by a later writer to a prophet. It is " Wherein
I find thee, therein will I judge thee." It does not
give any key to its context, notable as it is in itself.
Clement of Rome (ad Cor. viii.) has this :
" As I live, saith the Lord, I desire not the death of
the sinner so much as his repentance " (this is from
Ezek. xviii.), adding also a good sentence : " Repent ye,
O house of Israel, of your iniquity. Say unto the
children of my people : If your sins be from the earth
even unto the heaven, and if they be redder than scarlet
and blacker than sackcloth, and ye turn unto me with
your whole heart and say ' Father,' I will hearken unto
you as unto a holy people." This is not in our texts
of Ezekiel : it may be a later amplification thereof.
Clement of Alexandria also quotes : " If your sins,"
etc., in *Pædag.* i. 10, as from Ezekiel. Compare also
his *Quis Dives salvetur*, 39, where he has the former part
of the passage, somewhat expanded. Under the head-
ing of *Eldad and Medad* I gave a prophetical passage
which Clement of Rome and the Second Epistle both
use. I am inclined to think that Resch may be right
in assigning it, as well as that which has just been cited,
to the apocryphal Ezekiel. The terms of it, as was
said above, seem more appropriate to Israel in Exile
than to Israel in the Wilderness. Resch assigns'
several other quotations in 1 and 2 *Clement* to the
same book, but with less plausibility.

The *Lives of the Prophets* (Pseudo-Epiphanius) have
several legends about Ezekiel; more, in fact, than
about any other of the prophets. He was of the land
of Sarira. The chief of the people in the place of his
sojourn in Babylon slew him because he was rebuked
by him for the worship of idols. He gave a sign to the
people that they should observe the river Chobar ;
if its water failed they were to expect the sickle of
desolation (a designation of Antichrist which we have
had already) to the ends of the earth : if the water
overflowed, that signified their return to Jerusalem :
and this happened. He is buried in the land of the
Syrians, and many resorted to his tomb in prayer.

Upon the occasion of such a concourse of Jews, the
Chaldeans feared a rising and plotted to come and
slaughter them. The prophet made the waters of the
river stand, that the Israelites might cross it and
escape. Their pursuers were drowned.

By his prayer, in a time of famine, he procured them
a sudden and miraculous supply of fish, and raised many
to life who had died. When their enemies attacked
them, he obstructed them by portents and they ceased
from troubling.

In Babylon he judged the tribes of Dan and Gad,
who were impious and persecuted the followers of the
Law, and wrought this miracle, that serpents devoured
their children and their cattle. And he predicted that
on their account the people should not return to
Jerusalem, but should be in Media until the end of their
transgression. And of those tribes was the man who
slew him : for they withstood him until the day of his
death.

What I have omitted in this abstract is a description of Ezekiel's tomb, and some traits evidently taken
from the canonical book. Most of what I have given
does not appear anywhere else : it may be based on
current tradition. The one point that does occur
elsewhere is Ezekiel's violent death. In the Syriac
Acts of Philip, the *Apocalypse of Paul* and the *Imperfect
Work on Matthew* (a remarkable Arian commentary
of the fifth century, rather rich in apocryphal quotations), it is said that he was dragged by his feet upon
the mountains until his brains were dashed out. Origen
also, in a passage to be quoted later (under *Zechariah*),
speaks of Ezekiel's martyrdom as being related in
apocryphal writings. In almost the only picture I know
of his death (fifteenth-century glass in St. Martin's, Coney
Street, York) he is hung by his armpits on a gibbet
and two men are tormenting him. This has no old
authority behind it that I can discover.

The analogy of the *Ascension of Isaiah* and the *Paralipomena of Jeremiah* suggests the possibility that in the
apocryphal *Ezekiel* the climax of the story was that

Ezekiel was put to death, perhaps by being dragged
over the mountains, as a result of uttering a Christian
prophecy, it may be the prophecy or parable about
the heifer.

DANIEL

Of Daniel I will take leave to say but little. Imbedded somewhere in the apocryphal *Seventh Vision*
or *Apocalypse*, of which we have versions in Greek,
Coptic, Armenian and other tongues, there may lurk
quite old elements : but, as we have them, the texts
are of very late complexion. There are legendary lives
of Daniel, too, *e. g.* one in Persian : and there is a
Passion of Daniel and the Three Children in Greek,
which tells how all four were beheaded by a tyrant
Atticus, a successor of Nebuchadnezzar. It is a curious
tale, to which little attention has been paid. There
is an abstract of it, with a picture, in the great illustrated Menology of Basil in the Vatican.

If I am asked which of these documents is meant
by the " pseudepigrapha of Daniel " in the lists, I
should hazard the answer that it is an old form of the
Seventh Vision.

The *Dreambook* or *Somniarium* of this prophet is also
quite old : it exists in many forms and languages.
Usually it is an alphabetical list of objects that are
likely (in the compiler's opinion) to be dreamt about,
with an indication of the meaning of each. A short
preface opens it, the gist of which is that the princes
and all the people of Babylon begged Daniel to explain
to them the dreams which they saw, and he sat down
and wrote this book.

We pass to the minor prophets. Only three names
out of the twelve seem to have attracted the makers
of apocryphal books : Habakkuk, Zephaniah, Zechariah.

HABAKKUK

Habakkuk's apocryphon, whatever it was, is lumped
together in the lists with those of Baruch, Ezekiel and

Daniel, and we gather nothing of its nature or its
length. There is only one fact known to me which
can be imagined to throw any light upon it, and that
is that in the LXX the addition to Daniel known as
the *Story of Bel and the Dragon* has a title : " From the
prophecy of Hambacum the son of Jesus, of the tribe
of Levi." This is found only in the unique Chigi MS.
of the true Septuagint version of Daniel (all other
Greek MSS. giving that of Theodotion) and in the
Ambrosian (Milan) Syriac Hexaplar MS. It stands,
then, very much alone, but there is no sound reason
for doubting that the story which it heads did occur
in a book attributed to Habakkuk. Indeed, if we
compare the LXX and Theodotion versions of v. 33,
we shall see something that may serve to confirm the
title. Theodotion has : " And Habacum the prophet
was in Judæa," etc. The LXX : " And it came to
pass on the sixth day that Hambacum had bread
broken up in a bowl," etc. In the former he is introduced as the prophet, and it is found necessary to say
where he was : in the latter he and his abode appear
to be already known to the reader. It is a slight indication, but I think it is a real one. If the Septuagint's
title may be trusted, we infer that the Habakkuk book
had a considerable narrative element in it.

The Pseudo-Epiphanian *Lives of the Prophets* have a
fairly copious account of Habakkuk. They say : He
was of Bethzouchar, of the tribe of Simeon (this disagrees with the Chigi MS.). When Nebuchadnezzar
invaded the land he fled to Ostrakine, and was a
sojourner in the land of Ismael. He returned later to
his home and ministered to the reapers : as he cooked
food for them he prophesied to his own people and
said, " I shall go to a land far off and return quickly :
but if I tarry, take the food to the reapers," and he
was at Babylon and gave the dinner to Daniel in the
den of lions, and returned, and told no man what had
happened : but he understood that the people would
quickly return from Babylon to Jerusalem.
He gave a sign to them of Judæa, that they should

see a great light shining in the temple, and so should
see the glory of God : and concerning the end of the
temple, that it should come to pass by means of a
western nation : then the veil of the Daber should be
rent into two pieces and the capitals of the two pillars
taken away, and no man should know where they
were, but they should be carried by angels into the
wilderness, where the tabernacle was set up at first.
And in them shall the Lord be known at the end, and
shall enlighten them that are persecuted by the serpent,
as it was from the beginning. And the Lord shall save
them from darkness and the shadow of death and shall
be in an holy tabernacle. This prophet prophesied
much about the coming of the Lord; he died two
years before the return of the people from Babylon,
and was buried with honour in his own field.

Solomon of Basrah (thirteenth century) says : " The
Jews stoned him in Jerusalem."

Some of the above matter has the air of being extracted from a book of prophecy ; and it is more detailed
by far than the accounts of some other prophets, *e. g.*
Zephaniah and Haggai; but I cannot feel at all con-
fident that it really does preserve pieces of the pseud-
epigraphs of Habakkuk.

ZEPHANIAH

For Zephaniah we are better off. In the first place
we have a definite title, *Apocalypse of Sophonias*, and a
stichometry—600 lines. We also have an express
quotation. Clement of Alexandria (*Str.*, v. 11, 77)
says : Is not this (a passage from an Epistle of Plato)
like what is said by Sophonias the prophet ? " And the
spirit took me up and carried me into the fifth heaven,
and I beheld angels that are called Lords (and their
diadem was set upon them in the holy spirit, and the
throne of each of them seven times *brighter* than the
light of the sun as it shineth), dwelling in temples of
salvation and singing hymns to God unspeakable,
Most High." This must, one would say, be an extract

from an account of a progress through the seven
heavens, such as we have in the *Ascension of Isaiah,*
the *Testament of Levi,* the Greek *Baruch Apocalypse,*
and the *Secrets of Enoch.* Each heaven, it is indicated,
is inhabited by a different order of angels : the Lords
(κυριότητεσ, dominations, of St. Paul) are in the fifth.
The passage does not exactly coincide with any other
description : there is, indeed, nothing very distinctive
about it except the mention of the Lords. Yet it does
tell us something of the nature of the book whence it
is taken.

We have also an *Apocalypse of Zephaniah* in a frag-
mentary state in two Egyptian dialects, Achmimic
and Sahidic. The larger piece is in Achmimic : of the
Sahidic there is but one leaf. The editor, Steindorff,
calls the Achmimic an " anonymous Apocalypse " ; it
is true that the name of Zephaniah does not occur in
it (as it does in the Sahidic), but the coincidences of
language between the two are numerous, and I believe
it is the settled conviction of most who have studied
the book (it is certainly my own) that the Achmimic
is part of the same text as the Sahidic.

In neither of them does Clement's extract occur.
But the text is very strangely dislocated and incoherent,
and one is tempted to believe that the pages of the
Greek manuscript which the translator was using were
not in the right order. Whether that is so or not, the
Egyptian version cannot represent the original very
faithfully.

The main points of the longer fragment are these.

It begins with a badly mutilated passage which I
interpret as a vision of a deathbed of a righteous man
(like that in the *Apocalypse of Paul*). Then, in company
with an angel, the seer goes through a city and beholds
two men walking together, two women grinding together, and one on a bed (cf. Lc. xvii. 34–36 : what
happens to them we do not learn). The whole earth
is seen like a single drop of water. Something is then
said of a vision of torment. Next he is taken to Mount
Seir, and sees the three wicked sons of the priest

Joatham, and the recording angels weeping over them. Then there is a vision of angels of torment, followed by a very obscure passage in which gates of brass and a lake of fire figure. A great and monstrous spirit— the Accuser—is seen, and the seer in terror prays to be delivered, as Israel, and Susanna, and the Three Children were delivered. The chief recording angel, Eremiel, appears and shows the prophet a roll in which all his sins—failures to visit the widow and orphan, or to admonish the children of Israel—are recorded, and another in which probably were his good deeds. But here is a gap of two pages, and we next find him escorted by angels in a ship to a heavenly land. (This feature is in the *Apocalypse of Paul*.) He meets the righteous, and also sees various forms of torment. Abraham, Isaac and Jacob intercede (daily) for the sinners. The text ends in a speech of an angel who is describing what will happen at the last day.

The single leaf, or rather page, of the Sahidic MS. (one side is almost wholly illegible) contains only a vision of angels tormenting a soul. There is also the line : " Verily I Sophonias beheld this in the vision." On the perished *verso* of the leaf a few words can be read, among which is " drop of water," a hint that we have here the text (see above) in which the whole earth is seen like a single drop of water. A good deal of the Coptic book is Christian or Christianized. Unless other pieces turn up, we shall not be able to say for certain whether it is identical with the book · which Clement had read ; but the chances are much in favour of an affirmative answer.

ZECHARIAH

The *Apocalypse of Zacharias* (Zacharias the father of John, as two of the texts call him) was 500 lines in length. The question of its character is bound up with the question whether the Minor Prophet or the father of John the Baptist was the putative author. A. Berendts, who wrote a special study on the subject

(1895), was decidedly of opinion that the father of John was meant, and that the book contained an expanded form of the narrative of Herod's slaying Zacharias which we now read in the latter chapters of the *Protevangelium* or *Book of James*. He thought, moreover, that in a Slavonic writing, which he translated, he had discovered the actual book named in the lists. This narrative is wholly legendary and not apocalyptic. The attention of Berendts had not been called to a passage—a note of Origen on Ephes. iv. 27—which was printed in 1902 in the *Journal of Theological Studies* (iii. 554). " We give place to the devil, or to the prevailing spirit that comes up upon us, when the guiding principle in us has not been filled with holy learning or saving faith and excellent thoughts which counsel us for the best : for according to Zacharias the father of John, ' Satan tabernacles over (or, we might say, hovers over) the climates (κλίματα, regions?, inclinations?) of the soul,' and such concessions to the worse things . . . challenge the devil to enter into our souls."

This sentence is not of a kind which would fit easily into such a narrative as Berendts has produced : it is rather such as might be looked for in an Apocalypse.

Certainly Origen does seem to have been acquainted with a writing about the father of John which we do not possess. A comment of his on Matt. xxiii. 35 says, " a tradition to this effect has come down to us," that Zacharias allowed Mary to take her place among the virgins in the Temple after the birth of Christ, on the ground that she was still a virgin, and that he was slain by the men of that generation as a transgressor of the Law, between the Temple and the altar. He also says, in the Latin version of his commentary on Matthew, " It is said in apocryphal writings that Isaiah was sawn in sunder, and that Zacharias was slain, and Ezekiel." Jerome on Matthew (xxiii. 35) may be drawing from Origen when he writes, " Others will have it that Zacharias the father of John is meant ; they prove from some dream of apocryphal *writings* (he generally calls them *somnia* or *deliramenta apocry-phorum*) that he was slain because he prophesied the coming of the Saviour. This, having no Scriptural authority, can be as readily rejected as proved."

Coupled with the evidence of the note on Ephesians, these passages seem to support Berendts's view that the principal Zacharias-apocryph did relate to the father of John. There may very well have been prophetical passages in it.

I find it more difficult to agree with him in his identification of it with the Slavonic document. That, however, is worth summarizing here for the interest of the story.

In the fortieth year of Herod's reign, Joseph was warned by the angel Saphodamuel to flee into Egypt, where the family lived twelve months in the house of Alpheus, a man of God.

The massacre of the Innocents followed. Elizabeth fled with John. Zacharias was questioned about the child, and slain (as in *Protev.* xxii. ff.). Elizabeth was sheltered within a rock by Uriel, and fed.

After four months Gabriel brought Jesus to the Temple, and Uriel brought John : Michael and Raphael also came; and in the midst appeared God, and the corpse of Zacharias. God breathed life into it. Jesus made a spring of water rise up in the Temple and from it baptized John, and Zacharias.

Thereafter Zacharias fell asleep again and was buried by the angels before the altar. Gabriel and Uriel bore away Jesus and John. The story concludes with the weaning of John, and his life in the wilderness, and the return from Egypt.

That it is an old tale is more than likely, for it seems a sound view that it has been incorporated into the *Protevangelium* and not extracted from it. But it seems to belong rather to the John Baptist cycle of legend than to that of Zacharias; and in the book we are seeking for, Zacharias ought to be the centre of interest, and not, as here, a rather subordinate figure. To put the matter in another way, this legend strikes me rather as the beginning of a life of John than as the conclusion of a life of his father.

We have thus no clear evidence that there was an apocryphal book of the minor prophet Zechariah.

A story given by Sozomen (lib. ix. *Hist. Eccl.*) of the finding of the body of Zechariah in his time shall be mentioned, only to be dismissed.

It is to the effect that, with the body, the remains of a child in princely robes and crown were found; and when questions were asked as to the meaning of this, Zacharias Abbot of Gerara produced an un-canonical Hebrew book, in which it was recorded that · on the seventh day after King Joash had slain Zechariah (the son of Jehoiada) his favourite child died : he recognized that this blow was a divine judgment, and had the boy buried in the prophet's grave. The story does not concern our Zechariah, and the book, whatever it was, was not supposed to be written by any one of the name.

BARUCH

Baruch is the only other name in the lists which remains to be dealt with. We have plenty of books attributed to him besides that in our official Apocrypha : there is the Syriac Apocalypse and the Greek one (both of which are to be found in Dr. Charles's *Pseudepigrapha*), and also the *Rest of the Words of Baruch* or *Paralipomena of Jeremiah*, which has been edited by Dr. Rendel Harris : a translation of the Armenian version is in Issaverdens' collection. Justin the Gnostic—a heretic only known from the treatise of Hippolytus—had a book setting forth his peculiar system, in which an angelic being named Baruch figured, and the book bore his name; but that is hardly relevant here. There is an Ethiopic Apocalypse never printed (Brit. Mus., Add. MS. 16,223) which, Dillmann says, deals in part with the history of the Abyssinian Church.

There are also scattered quotations not traceable in the existing books of Baruch.

(*a*) Cyprian, *Testimonia* iii. 29 (not in all MSS.), has

this citation from Baruch : " For the time shall come
when ye and those that come after you shall seek me,
desiring to hear a word of wisdom and understanding,
and shall not find it. But nations shall desire to see
a wise man, and it shall not happen to them. Not
that the wisdom of this world shall be lacking or shall
fail the earth, neither shall the word of the law be
wanting to the world. For wisdom shall be among a
few that keep watch and are silent and talk with one
another in quiet, because some shall be afraid of them
and fear them as evil men. But these shall not even
believe the word of the law of the Most High, and others
gaping with their mouths shall not believe and shall
believe, and shall be contradicting and contrary, and
obstructing the spirit of truth. And others shall be
wise with the spirit of error and uttering *their own
words* as the sayings of the Most High and the Mighty,
and others shall be † personal of faith † (*personales
fidei*) : others capable and strong in the faith of the
Most High and hateful to *him that is* strange *thereto*."
   The corrupt words perhaps ought to have the meaning
" weak in faith " : I do not see how to mend them,
unless *personales* is a too literal rendering of διαφωνοῦντεσ
(" = failing "), which seems not unlikely. As Rendel
Harris remarks, this is like a passage in *Baruch* (*Syriac
Apoc.* xxxiii.) : " For not many wise shall be found at
that time, and they that understand shall be few, but
they that know shall for the most part keep silence.
   36. " And many shall say to many at that time :
Where hath the multitude of understanding hidden itself,
and whither hath the multitude of wisdom removed ? "
   (*b*) There is also a Baruch quotation in an old anti-
Jewish dialogue, the *Altercation of Simon and Theophilus*.
" How then did he, near the end of his book, prophesy
concerning His birth, and the habit of His raiment,
and His passion and resurrection, saying : This mine
anointed, my chosen, is called the offspring of (*lit.*
darted *or* thrown from : *jaculatus*) an undefiled womb,
and was born and suffered ? " The context of the
passage suggests to me that this citation was to be

understood as coming from the "deutero-canonical"
Book of Baruch in our Apocrypha. It may have been
a Christian addition to the end of Chapter iii., where
words occur which are regularly quoted as a prophecy
of the Incarnation.

(c) In Solomon of Basrah's *Book of the Bee* (ed.
E. A. W. Budge, 1886 : c. xxxvii. p. 81) we read, "*The
Prophecy of Zaradosht concerning our Lord.* This Zaradosht is Baruch the scribe." The prophecy is uttered
to the disciples of Zaradosht, the King Gushnasp
(Hystaspes) and Sasan and Mahmad. The Virgin-birth,
crucifixion, descent into hell, resurrection, ascension,
and second coming are predicted, and in answer to a
question of Gushnasp, Zaradosht says, "He shall
descend from my family. I am he and he is I; he
is in me and I am in him," and more to the same
effect. I do not know any other source which identifies
Baruch with Zoroaster.

Of these passages I think the first, from Cyprian, is
the only one that can be counted as a possible fragment
of a lost book.

EZRA

With a word about Ezra, Esdras, we actually end
our treatment of the lists. The book which they name
is, we may be sure, that known as 4 *Esdras*, or 2 *Esdras*
of the Apocrypha, which, with *Enoch*, is the most
famous of all apocryphal Apocalypses, and need not
be described here. I should, however, just like to
put on record a caution against what I believe to be
a misapprehension about it.

In the opening words (iii. 1) the supposed author
describes himself as " I Salathiel, who am also Esdras,"
and this has served critics as an argument in favour
of the thesis that the book is composed of a plurality
of documents welded together by a final editor, and
that one of these—the principal one—was an *Apocalypse
of Salathiel.* But I believe I have found evidence to
show that there was a Jewish tradition which identified
Esdras with Salathiel independently of this book.

Epiphanius (*on the Twelve Gems*) speaks of an " Esdras the priest—not that Esdras who was called Salathiel, whose father was Zorobabel, which Zorobabel was son to Jechonias." Epiphanius—who is wrong, by the way, in his genealogy—nowhere shows any knowledge of 4 *Esdras*. It is evident from what he says, and from other sources, that the name Esdras was supposed to have been that of several persons; one authority definitely states that Esdras the prophet, the author of 4 *Esdras*, and Esdras the scribe, the author of the canonical *Ezra*, lived about 100 years apart : also, 4 *Esdras* is dated, in its opening words, in the thirtieth year of the ruin of the city (530 B.C.), whereas Ezra the scribe belongs to the middle of the next century. The equation of Salathiel with Esdras is based, I believe, upon 1 Chron. iii. 17, where we read, " and the sons of Jeconiah, Assir, Salathiel his son " : and Assir, in despite of phonetic laws, was thought to be, or was forcibly assimilated to, the name Ezra : Assir and Salathiel being taken as two names for one man.

Further details may be read in two articles of mine in the *Journal of Theological Studies* for 1917 and 1918. The matter is of some little importance, because, if my view is correct, it does away with the only formidable argument in favour of the dissection of 4 *Esdras* into a congeries of documents.

The first two and last two chapters of the Latin version of 4 *Esdras* as they stand in our Apocrypha are later accretions. Chapters i., ii. are an independent Christian Apocalypse, surviving only in Latin. Chapters xv., xvi. are prophecies of woes conceived in the spirit of the Old Testament prophets and the *Sibylline Oracles*. They nowhere contain the name of an author : a small fragment has recently been found in Greek among the Oxyrhynchus papyri; otherwise they are preserved only in Latin.

There are several later Apocalypses of Esdras. One in Greek, edited from a single Paris MS. by Tischendorf (*Apocalypses Apocryphæ*) : one in Latin, printed by Mercati (*Studi e Testi* 5, 1901), and also by Bratke in a German periodical—I think the *Theol. Litteratur-Zeitung*—from different MSS. Both Greek and Latin contain visions of the next world, and represent some rather older document, but neither is specially interesting. To them probably applies the condemnation by Nicephorus Homologeta (*cir.* 850) of an *Apocalypse of Esdras*. An Ethiopic Apocalypse (Brit. Mus., MSS. Æth. 27, 61) has not been printed. One in Syriac (ed. Baethgen, 1886, *Zeitschrift für Alttest. Wissenschaft*) has passages about Islam, and must be late in its present form. In Issaverdens' translation of Armenian apocrypha are some *Inquiries of Esdras concerning Souls*—a dialogue with an angel, imperfect at the end, of Christian complexion.

There is also a series of prognostics—*Kalandologia* and *Brontologia*—predicting the character of the year from the day of the week on which it begins, or telling of auspicious days, or what thunder portends at various times of year. More of these are ascribed to Esdras (the "Erra Pater" of *Hudibras*) than to any one else, but Shem, David and Ezekiel also occur as authors of them. They are to be found in Greek and in several Western vernaculars, and are comparable to the dream-book of Daniel and the magical and alchemical books current under the names of Abel, Seth, Moses, Miriam, Solomon.

As to a Christian passage supposed by Justin Martyr to have been excised from the text of Ezra by the Jews, see Rendel Harris's *Testimonies*, I.

We have now done with prophets, and revert to kings.

HEZEKIAH

The Testament of Hezekiah is once mentioned, by George Cedrenus, who says (p. 120, Paris) : " In the *Testament of Ezekias* king of Judah, Esaias the prophet says that Antichrist has power for three years and seven months, which is 1290 days. And after Antichrist is cast into Tartarus the Lord of all things, Christ our God, comes, and there is also a resurrection

and retribution for good and evil deeds." This occurs
in a collection of rather incoherent paragraphs, roughly
in chronological order, which deal with Old Testament
history, and are followed by a more connected narrative
going over the same ground. The quotation coincides
with a passage in the *Ascension of Isaiah* (iv. 12 ff.),
" and he shall bear sway three years and seven months
and twenty-seven days," etc. The number of days
(1334) disagrees with Cedrenus. In *Asc.* i. 2, 4 we have
an apparent reference to visions of Hezekiah, who
summons Manasseh " in order to deliver unto him the
words of righteousness which the King himself had
seen (in his sickness, i. 4, 13), and of the eternal
judgments and the torments of Gehenna," etc. Dr.
Charles and others have not unnaturally thought of
the *Testament of Hezekiah* as a writing, part of which
at least has been incorporated into the *Ascension*.
This part is supposed by Dr. Charles to comprise
Asc. iii. 13*b*. to iv. 18—a prediction of Christ and
Antichrist. The *data* in *Asc.* i. imply that Hezekiah
had certain revelations about these matters in his
sickness in the fifteenth year of his reign. And the
" testamentary " part of the book would be, according
to analogy, his telling these revelations, at the end of
his life, to his son Manasseh. Manasseh remains un-
affected by them, and Isaiah tells Hezekiah that
Manasseh will do evil and will put him, Isaiah, to death,
and that God will not allow Hezekiah to slay Manasseh
in order to prevent this crime. That is the substance
of *Asc.* i.

The writer of the *Opus Imperfectum* on Matthew, in
his first homily, when treating of the genealogy of
Christ, and particularly of the name of Manasseh,
quotes something which does not exactly correspond
with our texts of the *Ascension*, but comes very near
them.

" When Ezechias had fallen sick at one time and
Esaias the prophet had come to visit him, Ezechias
called his son Manasses, and began to command him
that he ought to fear God, and how to rule his kingdom,

and much else. And Esaias said to him : ' Verily, thy words go not down into his heart; but it must also befall that I should be slain by his hand.' Ezechias, hearing that, wished to slay his son, saying, ' It is better for me to die without a son than to leave such a son, who should both provoke God, and persecute the saints.' And Esaias the prophet hardly restrained him, saying, ' God will make this thy counsel of none effect,' seeing the piety of Ezechias, that he loved God more than his own son." He then gives the story of Manasseh's captivity, sufferings, and deliverance, in words which coincide with those of the *Apostolic Constitutions* (ii. 22) and are pretty evidently taken from them; he omits the *Prayer of Manasses* which is given there. (Very shortly afterwards he quotes the story of King Amon, which is also in the *Apostolic Constitutions* (ii. 23) : and elsewhere he uses that book. So we need not doubt that the *Constitutions* (or *Didascalia*) are his source for the latter part of his account of Manasseh.) In the above passage about Hezekiah and Isaiah it is to be noted (*a*) that the king's illness is specially mentioned, and (*b*) that his words (" It is better for me," etc.) do not occur in the *Ascension*.

Later on, in *Hom*. 33, he says that the Jewish people " bore false witness, in the person of those who slew the prophets, especially against Esaias, before King Manasses, saying : He calls your princes men of Sodom and the people of Israel men of Gomorrha : he blasphemes, *saying* that he has seen the Lord Sabaoth, whereas God says : No man shall see my face and live. Wherefore also he was sawn with a wooden saw." This passage from the *Opus Imperfectum* is not adduced, I think, by any of the editors of the *Ascension*. It is in substance *Asc*. iii. 8–10, v. 1, the order of the two accusations being reversed, and the text shortened by the Homilist. So he knew a part of the *Asc*. which does not, *ex hypothesi*, belong to the *Testament* (iii. 13*b*–iv. 18). Indeed, we ought to credit him with knowing the whole of *Asc*., for we have fragments of a Latin version covering all the book, preserved in a

G

fifth or sixth century MS. of Arian origin : and our
Homilist was an Arian of the fifth century, who wrote
in Greek.

I am myself very much puzzled by this question of
what the *Testament of Hezekiah* was. There must have
been more of it, one is inclined to say, than Dr. Charles
assigns to it. Did it perchance go on to relate the
destinies of Manasseh, and was it the source of his
Prayer ? I hardly think so. The *Apostolical Constitutions (Didascalia)* are our earliest evidence for the
Prayer, and my reading of them suggests that they are
using an interpolated text of *Chronicles*. There is
nothing Christian in the *Prayer*, and the *Testament* as
quoted by Cedrenus is Christian. Or is " *Testament of
Hezekiah*" an alternative title for what we call the
Ascension of Isaiah ? It would be a strange one, and
it has left no other trace. Yet Cedrenus is not likely
to have invented it.

My acceptance of Dr. Charles' view is impeded by
the strong case with which Professor Burkitt (in his
Schweich Lectures on Apocalypses) has made out in
favour of the unity of the whole *Ascension*. He is
seconded by Mr. Vacher Burch (*Journal Theol. Studies*,
1918).[1] He does allow, it is true, for the interpolation

---

[1] Mr. Burch's article seeks to show from a passage in *Asc.*
iv. 21, 22, that the *Ascension* is avowedly based upon the primitive Christian book of *Testimonies* (which Dr. Rendel Harris
and he have investigated with such interesting results). The
words on which he bases his speculation are these (iv. 21) :
" and the descent of the Beloved unto Sheol, behold, it is written
in that section where the Lord saith, ' Behold, my son will
understand ' (Isa. lii. 13). And all these things, behold, they
are written in the parables of David," etc. (here follows an
enumeration of prophetical books). The " section " referred
to is, according to Mr. Burch, a section of the book of *Testimonies*. But surely the two verses which immediately precede
his quotation tend to show that it is a section of the canonical
Book of Isaiah which is being cited. They run thus : (19) " and
the rest of the words of the vision are written in the vision of
Babylon (Isa. xiii.). (20) And the rest of the vision regarding
the Lord, behold, it is written in the parables according to my
words which are written in the book which I publicly prophesied."
Mr. Burch takes no notice of these two verses, which I am afraid

of a passage in Chapter xi. which is absent from two of
the versions. He does not write on the question of the
Testament.

I believe that with our present lights we cannot get
further than saying that there was a book known as
the *Testament of Hezekiah*, which contained revelations
made to the King in his sickness; that these were
Christian in character, and that the substance of a
good part of them and of the book as a whole is preserved in the first five chapters of the *Ascension.* But
whether it was incorporated into the *Ascension* or
developed out of it remains for me uncertain.

There is other mythical matter connected with
Hezekiah's name. He is said to have burned the
medical and magical books of Solomon, and to have
obliterated the secrets, of cures, and the like, which
had been engraved on the Temple gates. Others relate
that these secrets were written on the wall of his
chamber, and that when he turned his face to the
wall (Isa. xxxviii. 2) it was to consult them. Cedrenus
is one of those who tells of the burning of the books,
and it is also he who, when treating of Hezekiah's
reign, tells the story of the man who gave all his
property away, relying on the promise that God would
repay him with increase : and of his disappointment
and subsequent conversion, which fell out on this wise.
He resolved to go to Jerusalem and inquire of God,
or rather arraign His justice for deceiving him. As he
went he met two men disputing about a stone they
had picked up, and appeased their quarrel by buying
it of them at the price of his only two remaining coins.
On arriving at Jerusalem he showed the stone to a
goldsmith, who, on seeing it, worshipped. It was a
gem that for three years had been missing from the
high priest's breastplate, and a great price would be

given for it. Meanwhile an angel appeared to the high priest and told him that that day the lost stone would be brought to him by a man to whom he was to give a great sum of money, and then smite him lightly on the face and say to him, " Be not doubtful in thy heart, and disbelieve not the Scripture that says, ' He that hath pity on the poor lendeth unto the Lord.' " So it was done. The man left all the wealth in the Temple, and went home, to doubt no more.

This story has made its way into Christian books—the Ethiopic romance of Clement (ed. Budge, *Contendings of the Apostles*), where it is told of Clement's father; and it may be read, rendered from Latin, in S. Gaselee's *Stories of the Christian East.* Cedrenus tells it, as I said, under Hezekiah's reign,[1] and along with the story of Tobit. I infer that he took it from a Jewish apocryphon—not impossibly that of Ezekiel, which its parable-character would suit well enough.

[1] In the Chronicle of Georgius Hamartolus (ed. de Muralt, 1859: lii. p. 154) the story is also given : it is there placed between the reigns of Joash and Amaziah.

QUOTATIONS

It now remains to collect certain anonymous quotations, purporting to be Scriptural, which appear in the works of early Christian writers. I can hardly hope that I have not missed some such, but probably all that are of first-class interest will be found here.

A word of caution is necessary. Whoever has read Dr. Rendel Harris's *Testimonies* (Part I.) must recognize that when we encounter passages seemingly conflated out of texts from the Old Testament, there is a possibility that we may be dealing with extracts from an early Christian selection of *logia* or *testimonies* from the prophets, or with erratic renderings of texts that we know in other forms, not with citations from lost writers. I suspect that this is the case with a good many of the passages I have here put together, though their origin has not yet been tracked out.

The Apostolic Fathers come first.

Clement of Rome. *Ep. ad. Cor.* xxix. (after quoting Deut. xxxii. 8): " And in another place he says, ' Behold, the Lord taketh to Himself a nation from the midst of the nations, as a man taketh the firstfruits of his threshing floor : and there shall come forth out of that nation the holy of holies' (Neuter Plural)."

This is guessed by Gebhardt and Harnack to be a conflation of passages in Deut. (iv. 34, vii. 6, xiv. 2), Num. (xviii. 27), 2 Chron. (xxxi. 14), Ezek. (xlviii. 12), but these do not contain the whole, by any means. Resch would assign it to the apocryphal Ezekiel, along with the prophecy quoted above under *Eldad and Medad*, and with the next :

l. c. l. 4 : " For it is written, ' Enter ye into the

87

store-chambers for a little moment, until my anger and
wrath be overpast : and I will remember the good day
and will raise you up out of your coffins.'"
Here the first clause is found in Isa. xxvi. 20, and
the last, perhaps, in Ezek. xxxvii. 12, but there is not
exact agreement with either.

In xvii. 5 the words, " But I am the vapour from a
pot," are attributed to Moses. Dr. Rendel Harris has
pointed out that the real source is 1 Chron. xxix. 15.

xxvi. 2 : " He saith in a certain place, ' And Thou
shalt raise me up and I will give thanks unto Thee,'
and ' I laid me down and slept and rose up, for Thou
art with me.'"
The first quotation is not exactly to be found in the
Psalms, but the second is combined from Ps. iii. (iv.) 6
and xxiii. 4; I imagine Clement is quoting inexactly
from memory. He would be less likely to verify
quotations from the Psalms than from any other book.

xlvi. 2 : " For it is written : Cleave unto the holy,
for they that cleave to them shall be made holy."
Ps. xviii. 26 follows.

" Cleaving to the holy " is a phrase twice used by
Hermas, and Clement of Alexandria quotes Ps. xviii. 26
and then our passage, probably using the Epistle, which
he knew well. The words, " for if thou cleave to the
holy thou shalt become holy," are also in an early
tract of canons to which Hilgenfeld gave the name of
the *Two Ways, or Judgment of Peter*.

In " 2 Clement " xiii. 3 is a passage not marked as
a quotation, but reading like one : " But ye know that
already the day of judgment cometh burning like a
furnace, and certain of the heavens shall melt, and all
the earth, melting like lead upon the fire; and then
shall the secret and the manifest works of men appear."
The *Apocalypse of. Peter* is a likely source here; there
is a distinct resemblance to 2 Peter iii. 10.

Barnabas vi. 13 : " The Lord says : ' Behold, I make
the latter things as the first.'" To this end, therefore,
the prophet proclaimed : " Enter ye into a land flowing
with milk and honey, and have dominion over it."

Though inexact, neither clause goes far away from what may be found in the Bible.

vii. 4 : "What saith He in (by) the prophet? ' And let them eat of the goat that is offered at the fast for all the sins.' Give good heed. ' And let the priests alone all eat the intestine unwashed, with vinegar. . .'"

7 : (after quoting Lev. xvi. 7 *sq*. : "Take two goats," etc.). But what are they to do with the other? "Cursed, saith he, is the other." See how the type of Jesus is manifested : "And spit, all of you, upon it, and pierce it, and put the scarlet wool about its head, and so let it be cast into the wilderness."

We can hardly be wrong in reckoning this as a Christian interpolation into Leviticus, comparable to, but more serious than, that in the Psalm, "The Lord reigneth *from the Tree*," which runs through all the early centuries.

xi. 9 : "And again another prophet saith : And the land of Jacob was praised above all the earth. . . . 10. Then what saith He?". "And there was a river flowing from the right, and there came up out of it goodly trees, and whosoever eateth of them shall live for ever."

Apparently the two clauses are from a single source, which reminds one of Ezek. xlviii. 1–12, but is not the same.

xii. 1 : "Likewise again he defineth concerning the Cross in another prophet who saith : ' And when shall these things be accomplished? The Lord saith : When a tree (or timber) and wood shall lie down and arise, and when blood shall drop from a tree (or wood).' "

It has been thought that this is from 4 *Esdras* iv. 53, but of late opinion has been against that view, and, I think, rightly. Discussions of it may be found in Rendel Harris's *Rest of the Words of Baruch* and in my Introduction to 4 *Esdras*.

xvii. 6 : "For it is written : And it shall be, when the week is being accomplished, that the Temple of God shall be built gloriously in the name of the Lord."

This is like Dan. ix. 24 ff. Resch would attribute it to the apocryphal Ezekiel.

Clement of Alexandria, whom we have found to be
a rich source, is our next hunting-ground.

Protrepticus viii. *fin.*: " Hear again the prophet who
says : The sun shall fail and the heaven shall be
darkened, but the Almighty shall stand for ever : and
the powers of the heaven shall be shaken, and the
heavens shall be rolled up like a curtain, stretched out
and pulled in (for these are the words of the prophecy),
and the earth shall flee from the face of the Lord."

Many Biblical phrases are here, but the *ensemble* is
not Biblical, and an Apocalypse of an Old Testament
character does seem likely to be the source.

Protr. x. 98 : " A certain prophecy says that things
here (on earth) will be in an ill plight when they (men)
put their faith in statues."

Pædagogus III. viii. 44. The expression " intelligent
fire " (φρόνιμον πῦρ) is used. God " poured out a little
of that intelligent fire " upon Sodom. It is a phrase
which recurs in Clement and other writers, and which
I believe we owe to some apocryphal book. It means
a fire which distinguishes between the good and the bad.

The *Pistis Sophia* c. 115 speaks of " a very great,
very vehement, wise fire which will burn up sins."

Clem. Alex., *Eclogæ ex propheticis scripturis*, 26 :
" The fire is conceived of as a good power and mighty,
destroying the worse and preserving the better, for
which reason this fire is called in the prophets intelligent."
Cf. also 27.

Strom. vii. 34. 4 : " We say that the fire sanctifies
not the flesh but the sinful souls; *we do* not *mean* the
all-devouring ordinary fire, but the intelligent, that
penetrates the soul that passes through the fire."

Origen (*on Prayer*, 29) : " Rather the retribution of
their error takes place in them when they are delivered
to sufferings of dishonour or cleansed by the intelligent
fire, and in prison have the payment for every one of
their shortcomings exacted from them to the uttermost
farthing."

Origen (*on Ezekiel*, i. 3) : " What, O Apostle, is that
fire which tries our works? What is that fire so wise

that it keeps my gold . . . and only consumes the evil
I have done?"
Minucius Felix, *Octavius*, (viii.) 35. 3 : " There a wise
fire burns the members and refreshes them, consumes
and nourishes."
Testament of Isaac (Coptic, p. 41, Guidi) : " The river
of fire did not hurt the righteous, but the sinners, since
the fire was knowing them."
Id. Arabic (Barnes, ap. *Test. of Abraham*, p. 147) :
" And the river (of fire) had intelligence in the fire
thereof, that it should not hurt the righteous, but the
sinners only, burning them." The *Test. of Jacob* (ibid.) :
" The river of fire which is prepared to separate the
transgressors from the polluted (?)."
The *Apocalypse of Peter* had the conception of a river
of fire which at the last day all souls were to pass, and
which should spare the righteous and burn the sinners.
But I am inclined to think that it must have appeared
in a Jewish apocalypse before that, with the definite
description " intelligent fire."
Pæd. III. xii. 89 : " Good works," saith he, " are a
prayer acceptable to the Lord." Cf. Prov. xv. 8. It
is not unlike the quotation from the *Apocalypse of Adam*
in Barnabas (p. 1). Here also it occurs in conjunction
with passages from Isa. i.
Stromateis, II. vi. 28, 29. After quoting Isa. liv. 1,
he continues with words which are not in our texts of
the Hebrew or LXX : " Thou livedst in the enclosure
of the people, thy children were blessed in the tabernacles of the fathers. . . ." And he adds more plainly :
" Thou didst inherit the covenant of Israel." This
hardly ranks as apocryphal.
Str. III. xviii. 106 : " Makers of war, strikers with
their tails, according to the prophet."
Str. VII. xii. 74 : " The voice that says : ' Whomso-
ever I smite, do thou pity.' "
Excerpt. ex Theodoto, 10. In this and other sections
there is mention of the first-created angels (seven in
number, as we learn from Hermas and from the
Stromateis). They are higher than the archangels (12,

27). The word used is πρωτόκτιστοι : the idea occurs in Jewish writings, *e. g.* the *Pirke R. Eliezer* 4, where it is said that before God is spread a veil, and the seven first-created angels serve Him before the veil. This veil is spoken of in the *Exc. ex Theodot.* 38, and there is something like it in the *Testament of Isaac.* See also Clement's *Ecloga ex propheticis scripturis* 51, 52, 57, *Adumbr. in* 1 *Joh.*

Irenæus, *Apostolical Preaching* c. 43, after quoting " Jeremiah " : " Before the morning star I begat thee (Ps. cx.), and before the sun is his name (Ps. lxxii. 17)." And again he says : " Blessed is he who was there before the coming of man into being." Lactantius, *Div. Inst.* iv. 8, quotes as from Jeremiah : " Blessed is he who was, before he was born." On these passages see Rendel Harris's *Testimonies,* I. 72, and Dean Robinson's forthcoming edition of the *Apostolical Preaching.*

Hippolytus (*on Antichrist,* 15) : " And another prophet also saith : He shall gather together all his power from the rising of the sun unto the going down thereof : whom he hath called and whom he hath not called shall go with him : he shall make the sea white with the sails of his ships and the land (plain) black with the shields and the weapons : and every one that shall meet him in battle shall fall by the sword."

Hilgenfeld thought this was from the *Apocalypse of Peter,* but we may now be sure that that book said very little, probably nothing, about Antichrist ; and the words have all the flavour of an Old Testament prophecy. My own attribution would be to the *Apocalypse of Elias.*

Tertullian (*on the Resurrection of the Flesh,* 32) : " But that there may not appear to be a resurrection only of these bodies which are committed to graves, thou hast *it* written : ' And I will command the fishes of the sea, and they shall vomit up the bones that are devoured, and I will make joint come to joint and bone to bone.' " The last words are like those of Ezek. xxxviii. 7, and the whole passage agrees in substance with *Enoch* lxi. 5, but not in wording. Tertullian does not very often quote apocrypha,[1] but the pseudo-Ezekiel, we have seen, is known to him; this may be from it.

HYSTASPES

A book of a somewhat different kind from those we have been considering has to be noticed now. It is the *Prophecy of Hystaspes*, a *soi-disant* pagan prophetical book of the same general character as the *Sibylline Oracles* (of which, it is hardly necessary to say, a large corpus, wholly Jewish or Christian, exists). The supposed author, Hystaspes, Hydaspes, Gushtasp, is described as an ancient Persian king, contemporary with Zoroaster. Agathias (ii. 24) says that Zoroaster was ."in the time of Hystaspes," but that it was uncertain to him whether this was the father of Darius or some other Hystaspes. He speaks on the authority of the Persians of his own time (middle of the sixth century). In passing, I remind the reader that a Christian prophecy of Zoroaster, mentioned above under Baruch, is addressed to his disciple Gushnasp. Of Hystaspes, Ammianus Marcellinus (xxiii. 6, 32) has this to say: "Hystaspes, a most wise King, father of Darius. He, while boldly exploring the hidden parts of Upper India, came upon a lonely forest region whose still quietude was peopled by the wisest of the Brachmani: from them he learnt, so far as he was able, the system of the course of the world and the stars, and the ritual of a fire-worship; and some part of his learning he infused into the minds of the Magi, by whom, along with the lore of predicting the future, it is handed down to later ages through the descendants of each." This passage does not show Hystaspes as the author of a written work; our evidence as to that is all derived from Christian sources. There are four passages.

Clement of Alexandria, *Str.* vi. 5. 42, 43 : " In addition to the *Preaching of Peter* this will be seen from

[1] He is generally known to have used *Enoch ;* and Mr. H. N. Bate has recently called my attention to a passage in his *de bono patientiæ*, xiii., in which he not only alludes to the *Ascension of Isaiah*, but also, undoubtedly, to the *Testament of Job*, chap. xx.

the words of the Apostle Paul, who says : Take also
the Greek books, consider the Sibyl, how she declares
the One God and the future. Take Hystaspes and
read him, and you will find the Son of God written
of far more distinctly and clearly, and how that many
Kings will array themselves against the Christ, hating
him and those who bear his name, and his faithful
ones, and his patience, and his appearing."

I agree with others who see in this a probable quotation from the ancient *Acts of Paul.* If it represents
Hystaspes at all faithfully, we have no choice but to
set down the book as Christian.

Justin Martyr, *Apology*, i. 20 : " And the Sibyl too,
and Hystaspes, said that there should be a dissolution
of corruptible things by means of fire."

Id. 44 : " (By the evil one's contrivance) death was
decreed against those who read the books of Hystaspes
or the Sibyl or the Prophets." The reason for this
decree will appear from the next passage.

Lactantius, *Divine Institutes*, vii. 19. 19 : " Hystaspes
also, who was a most ancient king of the Medes, from
whom the river took its name which is now called the
Hydaspes, left on record for posterity a wonderful
dream interpreted by a prophesying boy (*sub inter-
pretatione uaticinantis pueri*). He foretold that the
empire and name of Rome should be taken away out
of the world, *and that,* long before that race of Trojan
descent began to be."

This tells us something of the form of the book.
The king, I conjecture, had a symbolic vision, and a
marvellous child interpreted it to him, in the manner
of Daniel. Is it a faint late echo of this that we find
in mediæval times in the following story ? Each of the
Three Kings had a sign in his house before the birth
of Christ. In one case an ostrich laid two eggs, out
of which were hatched a lion and a lamb; in the
second, a balsam plant in the garden produced a flower,
out of which came a dove, and it announced that God,
the Maker of heaven, earth, and sea, the Saviour of all,
was born of a virgin; to the third King it befell that

his wife bare a son, who stood up on his feet and prophesied of Christ and foretold his own death after thirty-three days. The tale, which comes to us in Latin, is said in the MSS. to be drawn from a Greek writer, Germanus (? the Patriarch of Constantinople). The Latin will be found in O. Schade's *Narrationes de vita et conversatione B. Mariæ*, etc. (Königsberg, 1876), from a Giessen MS. I have also found it in MS. CCCC. 365 and in Cosin's Library at Durham (V. iv. 9). I believe representations of it are among the sculptures on the Cathedral of Ulm.

The last passage I know about Hystaspes is in what is known as the *Tübingen Theosophy* (Buresch. *Klaros*, p. 95). It is an epitome, contained in a MS. at Tübingen (a transcript of the burnt Strasburg MS. that contained the Epistle to Diognetus and other apologetic writings), of a fifth-century treatise in eleven parts, of which Books I. to VII. dealt with the True Faith, and VIII. to XI. were called *Theosophy*. "In the fourth (of the Theosophy) or eleventh (of the whole work) he produces oracles of Hystaspes, who was a most pious King, he says, of the Persians or Chaldeans, and therefore received a revelation of divine mysteries concerning the incarnation of the Saviour." He thus confirms, what the Clement-quotation suggested, that the book of Hystaspes was of Christian complexion.

APPENDIX

LADDER OF JACOB

BY way of appendix to the fragments of lost books I should like to add one or two notices of apocrypha which do not quite fit into the framework of the main part of the book.

The first of these is the *Ladder of Jacob*, which exists in two recensions in Slavonic, and was translated by Bonwetsch in the Göttingen *Nachrichten*, 1900 (p. 76). I depend upon his text for my rendering.

The first recension, contained in a single MS., rather mutilated, of 1494, in the Rumjançov Museum at Moscow, gives the most original text. The other has been printed by various Russian scholars and, like other apocrypha, is found in the text of the *Palæa*, or Old Testament History.

(Rec. 2) : Now Jacob went to his Uncle Laban, and he found a place and fell asleep there, laying his head on a stone, for the sun was set : and there he saw a vision.

(Rec. 1 *begins*) : And lo! a ladder was set up on the earth, whose top reached unto heaven. And the top of the ladder was a face as of a man, hewn out of fire. Now it had twelve steps up to the top of the ladder, and upon each step up to the top were two human faces on the right and on the left—twenty-four faces seen to their breast, on the ladder. But the middle face was higher than them all, which I saw made of fire, to the shoulder and the arm, very terribly, more than the twenty-four faces. And as I looked, behold, the Angels of God ascending and descending thereon : but the Lord was set above it, and he called me, saying : Jacob, Jacob. And I said : Here am I, Lord ; And he

said to me : The land whereon thou sleepest I will give
to thee and to thy seed after thee : and I will multiply
thy seed as the stars of heaven and as the sand of the
sea; through thy seed shall all the earth be blessed,
and they that dwell thereon, unto the last times, the
years of the end.   My blessing wherewith I have blessed
thee shall pour out from thee unto the last generation.
All in the east and the west shall be full of thy seed.

2. And when I heard it from above, fear and trembling
fell upon me, and I rose up from my dream.   And while
the Voice of God was yet in mine ears, I said : How
dreadful is this place ! this is none other but the house
of God, and this is the gate of heaven.   And I set up
the stone that was under my head for a pillar, and
poured oil on the top of it, and I called the name of
that place the house of God (*a line gone : Rec. 2 suggests
the supplement :* And I prayed to God and said) : Lord
God of Adam, of thy (creature?), and Lord God of
Abraham and Isaac my father, and of all whose ways
are right before thee, thou that sittest mighty upon
the Cherubim and upon the throne of the majesty,
of fire and full of eyes, as I saw in my dream ; that holds
the Cherubim with four faces, that bears the Seraphim
full of eyes, that bears the whole world under his arm,
and is borne of none.   Thou hast established the heaven
for the glory of thy name.   Thou hast spread out upon
the clouds of the heaven the heaven that flieth (resteth ?)
under thee, that under it thou mayest move the sun
and hide it in the night lest it be held for God : thou
hast ordained the way for the moon and the stars, and
her thou makest to wax and wane, but for the stars,
thou hast commanded them to pass over, lest these
also should be supposed gods.   Before the face of thy
majesty the six-winged Seraphim fear, and hide their
feet and their face with their wings, and with the others
they fly, and sing (*two lines gone : no help from Rec. 2,
which omits all this invocation*) Highest, with twelve
faces, many-named, fiery, lightning-formed, holy one !
Holy, Holy, Holy, Jao Jaova, Jaoel, Sabakdos, Chabod,
Sabaoth, Omlelech, Elaber, Ame(?) S'me Barech,

eternal king, strong, mighty, very great, long-suffering,
Blessed One, that fillest heaven and earth and the sea
and the abyss and all æons with thy glory. Hear
my song wherewith I have praised thee, and grant me
my petition for which I pray to thee, and show me the
interpretation of my dream. For thou art strong and
mighty and glorious, a holy God, the Lord of me and
of my fathers. (*This rather resembles the prayer in the
Apocalypse of Abraham, of which a translation is published in this series.*)

3. And while I yet spake my prayer, there appeared
a voice (!) before my face saying : Sarekl, prince of
them that rejoice (*or* of the servants), thou that art
over visions, go make Jacob to understand the interpretation of the dream which he saw, and show him
all things whatsoever he saw : but first bless him. And
the archangel Sarekl came to me, and I saw : it was a
face (*a line gone*) terrible. But I did not fear before
his look, for the face which I had seen in my dream . . .
was more than this, and I feared not the face of an
angel. And the angel said to me : What is thy name?
and I said : Jacob. But I (*read* he said to me) Thy
name shall not henceforth be called Jacob, but thy
name shall be like my name, Israel. And when I came
from Fandana (cf. *Apocalypse of Abraham*, 2) in Syria
to meet my brother Esau, he came to me and blessed
me, and called my name Israel, and told me not his
name until I adjured him, and then he told me : Because
thou wast . . . [*There is confusion here, it seems,
between the two incidents of the ladder and the wrestling.
I have wondered whether a dim reflection of the 'Prayer
of Joseph' is to be traced in this paragraph, but the text
is evidently in a bad state. Rec. 2 has merely the statement
that an angel came and said he was sent to interpret the
vision.*]

4. But this said he to me : The ladder which thou
sawest, which had twelve steps having two human faces
which changed their appearance—now this ladder is
this age, and the twelve steps are the times of
this age, and the twenty-four faces are the kings of

the lawless heathen of this age. Under these kings will be tried (*line gone : Rec.* 2 thy children's children and the line) of thy sons : they will rise up against the lawlessness of thy descendants and will lay this place waste through four descents (because ?) of the sins of thy descendants, and of the substance of the forefathers will be built this palace in the temple of the name of thy God and thy fathers (? the palace of the temple in the name. of the God of thy fathers); but through the wrath of thy descendants will it be desolate until (*Rec.* 2 in) the fourth descent of this age : for thou didst see four visions (*or* faces).

5. The first that stumbleth upon the steps . . . angels ascending and descending and faces in the midst of the steps : the Most High will raise up an heir of the descendants of thy brother Esau, and all the lords of the nations of the earth will accept it, who have done evil against thy seed, and will be given into his hand, and he will be hardly borne by them. But he beginneth to rule them with violence and to reign over them, and they cannot resist him, until the day when his decree goeth forth against them to serve the idols (*line gone*) and to all them that appear in such a cause, and so many . . . of thy race, so many to Thalkonagargael.

[Rec. 2 : The first that stumbleth upon the steps will be a king of thy neighbours and will do evil against thy seed; he will be unwillingly borne by them. But then beginneth he to rule over them, and with violence to reign over them, and they cannot resist him, and his decree groweth against them that they should worship idols and sacrifice to the dead (*the deified Emperor*) : and he speaketh to use force to all that are in his kingdom, which appear in such an accusation, so many to the Most High out of thy race, and so many to Thalkonagargael.]

6 (Rec. 1) : And know thou, Jacob, that thy seed shall be strangers in a strange land, and men will illtreat them with bondage and lay blows on them daily : but the people whom they serve will the Lord judge. When a king ariseth and fighteth, then will there be to

H

that place (*al.* when the Most High giveth his judgment to that place, he will lead forth) then will thy seed, even Israel, go forth out of the bondage of the heathen who ruled over them with violence, and will be set free from all reproach of their enemies. For this king is the head of every revenge and retribution of them that make attacks on thee, Israel. And the (at the?) end of the age (*sic*). For the miserable will rise and cry, and the Lord heareth them, and will be softened, and the mighty letteth himself pity their sufferings, because the angels and archangels pour out their prayers for the saving of thy race. Then will their women bear much fruit, and then will the Lord fight for thy race. *Here the oldest MS. ends.*

Rec. 2 : And know thou, Jacob, *etc. to* will the Lord judge, For the Most High will let himself pity, *etc. to* the saving of thy race, that the Most High may have compassion; then will their women bear much fruit, and then fighteth the Lord for thy race with terrible and great signs, for the bondage inflicted on them. Their full storehouses will be found empty of wine and of every fruit : their land will boil over with creeping things and every deadly thing. Earthquakes and much destruction will there be. Then will the Most High accomplish his judgment on that place, and will lead forth thy seed out of the bondage of the heathen which rule over them with violence, and they will be saved from the reproaches of their enemies. But the head of the king will be for (an object of) revenge : bitterly standeth he up against them, but they cry, and the Lord heareth them and poureth out his wrath upon the Leviathan the sea serpent, and smiteth the lawless Thalkon with the sword : for against the God of gods raiseth he up his pride. But then, Jacob, appeareth thy righteousness and that of thy fathers, and of them that shall be after thee, walking in thy righteousness : and then shall thy seed blow with the trumpet, and the whole kingdom of Edom shall perish, with all the kings and peoples of the Moabites.

Of these sections No. 4 seems to relate to the Temple

and the Exile, No. 5 more clearly to the Romans, No. 6 certainly to Egypt. What follows is Christian and is only in Rec. 2.

7. But whereas thou sawest angels descending and ascending upon the ladder, in the last times there will be a man from the Most High, and he shall desire to join the upper with the lower. Of him before his coming shall your sons and your daughters prophesy, and your young men shall see visions of him. For there shall be such signs *as these* at the time of his coming : a tree felled by the axe shall drop blood (cf. *Barnabas* xii. 1. *above*) ; boys of three months old shall speak rationally (*Sibylline Oracles, Testament of the Lord*, 4 *Esdras*) ; a child in its mother's womb shall proclaim his way (cf. Luke i.) ; a young man shall be as an old man. And then cometh the expected one, whose path will be perceived by no man. Then will the earth rejoice, because it hath received the glory of heaven. That which was above shall be below. And of thy seed shall grow up a royal root (*or* the root of a king) ; and he (it) shall increase and destroy the power of the Evil *one*, but he himself shall be a saviour of the heathen, and the rest of them that are weary, and a cloud which shadeth the whole world from the heat (Isa. xxxii. 2), for otherwise that which is disordered could not be put in order, if he came not : otherwise that which is below could not be joined to that which is above.

8. Now at his coming will images of brass (*al.* calves of brass) and stone and all graven things utter their voice for three days long. And they announce to the wise men and let them know what will befall (*or* is befalling) on earth, and by the star will they know the way to him, when they see him upon earth whom the angels see not above. Then will the Almighty be found in a body on the earth, and encompassed by the arms of a mortal, and he reneweth the state of man and quickeneth (Adam and) Eve that died through the fruit of the tree. Then will the deceit of the godless one be overcome, and all idols fall on their faces, for they will be put to shame by one who is adorned with

honour, because they made lying inventions. Thenceforth will they not have power to rule or to give prophecies, for their honour will be taken from them, and they will remain without glory. For he (the child) that is come taketh the power and might from them and recompenseth to Abraham the truth (righteousness) which he promised him. Then he (or For this child) roundeth off all that is sharp, and every rough thing maketh he smooth, and he casteth all unrighteousness into the depths of the sea : and he doeth wonders in heaven and on the earth. And he will be wounded in the midst of the house of the beloved (or the beloved house : *evidently* " the house of his friends," Zechariah xiii. 6). But when he is wounded, then also the saving and the end of all corruption draweth near. For they that have wounded him shall themselves receive a wound which shall not be healed for them for ever. But the wounded one shall all creatures worship, and upon him shall many hope, and everywhere, and among all the Gentiles, shall he be known. But they that have known his name shall not be put to shame. And his own might and his years shall not fail for ever.

The beginning of this section contains an undoubted reference to a document of uncertain date—the *Wonders in Persia* or *The Dispute at the Court of the Sassanidæ*, of which the sage Aphroditianus is the hero. In it the story is told at great length of the miracles, of speaking idols in particular, which happened in Persia at the time of our Lord's birth. This story may be a good deal older than the document in which it is imbedded. The whole text is best edited by Bratke in *Texte und Untersuchungen* (1899) : also by Wirth, *Aus Orientalischen Chroniken*.

I will note, in order to dismiss it, a passage of Epiphanius (*Hær*. xxx. 16), which has been supposed to refer to the *Ladder of Jacob*. Epiphanius says that the Ebionites made use of a book called the *Ascents of Jacobus* (ἀναβαθμοὶ Ἰακώβου) which represented him as inveighing against the Temple and its sacrifices. Nothing can be more obvious than that this refers to

James the brother of the Lord and not to Jacob : Lightfoot (*Galatians*, 276, 330, 367 etc.) was, I doubt not,
right in the main in his view that we have some relics
of the book in the Clementine *Recognitions* (Book I.) and
(perhaps) in the tale of Hegesippus about James's death.

THE LOST TRIBES

The first document that tells us anything of the legend
that the ten (or nine and a half) tribes were dwelling
together as a community in a remote and unknown
land is the passage in 4 *Esdras* xiii. 39 *sq.* The conception is also found in the *Apocalypse of Baruch*, lxxvii.,
lxxviii. It need not be traced out in full here; but
the subject is relevant to the present work, inasmuch
as there evidently was a writing (presumably Jewish)
which described the conditions under which the lost
tribes lived.

We find vestiges of it in various places. First come
two passages of the Christian poet Commodian, who,
whether he lived in the late third century, as was
commonly thought, or later, was acquainted with a
good many interesting apocryphal writings.

The first section of the second book of his *Instructions*
is entitled, " Of the hidden holy people of Almighty
Christ the living God." To translate his terrible Latin
literally is beyond me, but something like the sense can
be given. The first book of the *Instructions* ends by
telling how Antichrist comes and performs wonders.
The Jews, searching the Scriptures, cry aloud to the
Most High that they have been deceived by Antichrist.
Book II. begins : " The last holy hidden people, of whom
we know not where they dwell, are desired." It then
speaks, very obscurely, of the two and a half tribes
who are separated from the nine and a half, and returns
to its proper subject in line 21 : " But then the things
told in the law hasten to be fulfilled : Almighty Christ
comes down to His elect, who have been hidden from
us so long and grown to so many thousands. That
is the true heavenly people. The son dies not before

his father there, nor do they experience pains or sores growing in their bodies. They die in ripe age, resting in their beds, fulfilling the whole law, and therefore are they kept safe. They are (now) bidden to come over to the Lord from that region, and He dries up the river for them as He did before, when they passed over. Nor less does the Lord Himself come forth with them. He passes to our lands, they come with their heavenly King, and on their journey how shall I tell what God accomplishes for them? Mountains sink down before them, and springs break forth. All creation rejoices to see the heavenly people. And they hasten to rescue their captured mother.''

In the *Carmen Apologeticum* the same story is told. The Jews cry for help to God (ll. 934, 941): '' Then Almighty God, to fulfil all that I have spoken of, will bring forth a people hidden for a long time. They are the Jews who were cut off by the river beyond Persia, whom God willed to remain there until the end. The captivity caused them to be in that place : of twelve tribes, nine and a half dwell there. There is no lying nor any hatred : therefore no son dies before his parents : nor do they bewail their dead nor mourn for them after our manner, for they look for a resurrection to come. They eat no living thing among their food, but only herbs, for these are without shedding of blood. Full of righteousness, they live with unblemished bodies. The stars (*genesis :* perhaps lust is meant) excite no evil influence on them, no fever kindles them, nor fierce cold, because they purely obey all the law; to this we too should attain if we lived rightly; only death and toil are there, all else is without force.''

'' This people then, which now is laid up far away, will return to the land of Judah, the river being dried up. And with them God will come to fulfil the promises. All through the journey they exalt in the presence of God : everything grows green before them, all things are glad ; the creature itself rejoices to receive the holy ones. Everywhere springs break out of their own accord where the people of the Most High pass with the terror

of heaven. The clouds make a shadow for them that
they be not vexed by the sun, and lest they grow weary
the very mountains lay themselves flat." He goes on
to describe their irresistible might and rapid conquest
of the impious Antichrist.

The Ethiopic *Acts of St. Matthew* (tr. Budge, *Contendings of the Apostles*, ii. 112) tell how Peter and Andrew
met Matthew, and he told them that he had lately
been in the land called Prokumenos, which being interpreted is "Those who rejoice," and had found the
people Christian : in fact the Lord Himself constantly
visited them. He asked them how this came about.
Their answer was, "Hast thou not heard the story
concerning the nine tribes and the half tribe whom
God Almighty brought into the land of inheritance?
We are they. . . . As for gold and silver, we desire
it not in our country : we eat not flesh and we drink
not wine in our country, for our food is honey and our
drink is the dew. We do not look upon the face of
woman with sinful desire : our firstborn children we
offer as a gift to God, that they may minister in . . .
the sanctuary . . . until they be thirty years of age.
The water we drink floweth not from cisterns hewn
by the hand of man but . . . floweth from Paradise.
Our raiment is of the leaves of trees. No word of lying
hear we in our land, and no man knoweth another who
speaketh that which is false. No man taketh to wife
two women in our land, and the son dieth not before
his father, and the young man speaketh not in the
presence of the aged. The lions dwell with us, but they
do no harm to us nor we to them. When the winds
rise we smell the scent of Paradise, and in our country
there is neither spring nor cold nor ice, but there are
winds, and they are always pleasant."

That Commodian and the *Acts of Matthew* draw
ultimately from a common source seems clear. That
it was apocalyptic and Jewish is a safe conjecture :
but further than that I do not feel warranted in going.

An elaboration of the theme of the Utopian community
may be read in the *Narrative of Zosimas*, a hermit who

visited the secluded land and found it inhabited by the descendants of the Rechabites. He had to leave them because he suggested to his host that he should make an untruthful excuse. The text will be found in my *Apocrypha Anecdota*, I., and a translation in *Recently discovered MSS. (Ante-Nicene Christian Library)*.

OTHER LEGENDS

There are, of course, many other legends woven about the Old Testament history which may have been the themes of apocryphal books. Such, for instance, is the *Story of the Captivity*, which is current in Arabic. Two versions of it are accessible, one in the *Revue de l'Orient Chrétien* for 1910-11, the other in Amélineau's *Contes de l'Égypte Chrétienne*, II. It is a picturesque embroidery of the Bible story, of which Jeremiah is the hero, and it shows a knowledge of the *Paralipomena* of that prophet. Another is the Slavonic tale of Babylon, translated by Wesselovsky in the *Archiv für Slavische Philologie*, II. Neither could possibly be at all early in date, I think; the second might fairly be called a folk-tale. There are, besides, lives of Biblical heroes such as Joseph, David, and Job, in Arabic and other Eastern tongues, which have not as yet been looked into, and which may prove to contain old elements. But to stray much further than I have done into late workings-up of earlier matter would be inappropriate. I hope and believe that in the present collection not much that is of really old date will be found to have been passed over.

INDEX

Testaments. *See* Adam, Pro-
toplasts, Abraham, Twelve
Patriarchs, Patriarchs Three,
Isaac, Jacob, Job, Jesus
Christ, Moses, Hezekiah.
Testament of the Lord, 57, 101
Testament in Galilee, 57
Testimonia, 31, 84 *n.*, 87, 92
Thackeray, H., 53
Thalkon, Thalkonagargael, 99,
100
Theodotion, version of Daniel,
71
Theosophy, the Tübingen, 95
Timotheus of Constantinople,
40
Titus, Epistle of, 55
Toledo Cathedral, 11
Treves, Latin fragment on
Antichrist, 57
Tribes, the Lost, 103 ff.
Tubal Cain, 11
Tübingen Theosophy, the, 95
Twelve Patriarchs, Testaments
of the, 19 f., 29 f.

Ulm Cathedral, 95
Uriel, 2, 11, 22, 24, 25, 28, 31,
76

Vajoscha, Midrash, 59
Vassiliev, 47
Vincenti, A. von, 52

Wells Cathedral, 11
Wesselovsky, 106

York, glass at, 69

Zacharias. *See* Zechariah.
Zahn, Theodor, xiii, xiv
Zechariah in Matt. xxvii, 62;
Apocrypha of, 74 ff.; inven-
tion of, 77
Zephaniah, Apocalypse of,
72 ff
Zerubbabel, Book of, 59
Zoroaster identified with
Baruch, 79
Zosimas, Narrative of, 105
Zouche of Parham, Lord, 51

www.ingramcontent.com/pod-product-compliance
Lightning Source LLC
LaVergne TN
LVHW011403080426
835511LV00005B/389